THE
PHILOSOPHY OF
THE BED

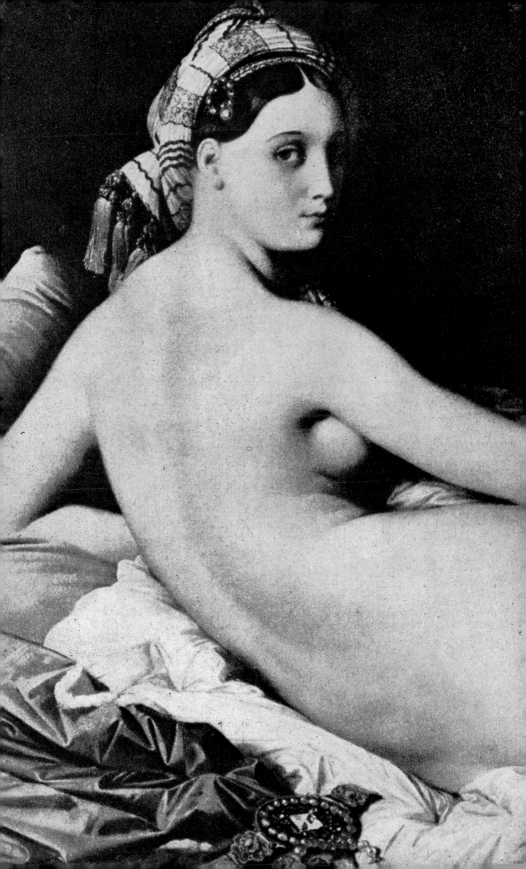

THE PHILOSOPHY OF THE BED

Mary Eden and Richard Carrington

SPRING BOOKS · LONDON

First published by Hutchinson
& Co. (Publishers) Ltd 1961

This edition published 1966 by Spring Books
Drury House - Russell Street - London WC2
Printed in Czechoslovakia by Tisk Brno
T 1733

*

For

PAT NEWMAN

and

YVONNE CAFFIN

*

Contents

Preface   13

1   Of Beds and their Furnishings   17

2   Some Aspects of Bedroom Life   32

3   Birth   44

4   Some Notable Beds   57

5   On Lying in Bed   65

6   Sleep   77

7   The Commerce of Love   88

8   The Art of Dying   101

Bibliographical Notes   109

Bibliography   115

Index   123

Figures

1   Solomon in bed   19

2   An Anglo-Saxon bed on wheels   21

3   A French 'mechanical bed'   23

4   A modern brass four-poster   25

5   Lady on a camp bed   36

6   The birth of Brahma   44

7   A Caesarean operation in the eighteenth century   45

8   Canadian cradles   55

9   'Angel cot' shown at the Great Exhibition   56

10   A Busy Night   70 & 71

11   A sixteenth-century hospital in Paris   102

THE BED, *my friend, is our whole life. It is there that we are born, it is there that we love, it is there that we die.*

If I had the pen of M. de Crébillon I would write the history of a bed, and what a record of adventures it would be—adventures thrilling and terrible, tender and gay. And what lessons could one not learn from such a record! And what morals could not be drawn for all mankind!

A young woman lies prostrated. From time to time she gasps, and then she groans, while the elders of the family stand round. And then there comes forth from her a little object, mewling like a cat, all shrivelled and lined. It is the beginning of a man!

Then here again are two lovers, flesh pressed to flesh for the first time in this tabernacle of life. They shudder but are transported with joy, and each feels the other's delicious nearness; then slowly their lips meet. They mingle in this divine kiss—this kiss which opens the gate to heaven on earth, this kiss which sings of human delights, promising all, and heralding the ecstasy to come. And their bed heaves as with the swell of the sea, whispers and sways, as if it were itself alive and joyful because it was seeing the consummation of the rapturous mystery of love.

And then again, my friend, think of death. For the bed is also the tomb of vanished hopes, the door that shuts out all, after once being the gateway to the world. What cries, what anguish, what suffering, what appalling despair, what groans of agony, what appeals to joy for-ever gone, has the bed not known? And what has it not seen of arms outstretched towards the past, of twisted bodies and hideous grins, of upturned eyeballs and contorted lips?

The bed is the symbol of life! The bed, indeed, is man!

From *Le Lit* by Guy de Maupassant
Translated and abridged by Richard Carrington

Preface

ABOUT a third of the normal human life is spent in the horizontal position, and from the earliest times man has recognized that this far from inconsiderable period should be passed as pleasurably as possible. Other members of the animal kingdom lie down to rest and to die, and some build elaborate structures to provide greater comfort in repose or a suitable environment for the reproduction of their young. These, of course, are beds of a kind, but the special type of bed we shall be mainly concerned with here is unique to man. It is, in fact, the object, raised on four legs and supporting a mattress and coverings of various kinds, which has become a familiar feature of every civilized home.

But, as the title of this book suggests, we do not intend to deal with the bed primarily as an article of furniture (although this aspect of the subject will be touched upon in passing). Beds are much more than material structures, with certain physical characteristics such as shape, style, and dimensions. They are the stage on which all the major biological activities of man are enacted. It is, of course, possible to be born in an aeroplane or to die in a car-smash, but these are hardly likely to be premeditated acts. Except in the most unusual circumstances we may all reasonably hope that the bed will be the place of our conception, our birth, the best part of our physical relaxation, and our death. Thus a book on the bed must attempt, however unpretentiously, to make some small contribution to social history.

We have few obvious credentials for undertaking a task of this kind. One of us has written briefly on the subject from the point of view of the social historian, and has therefore undertaken the greater part of the historical chapters. The other is known primarily as a writer on natural science and has thus concentrated mainly on the

13

biological aspects of the theme. Our only other qualifications are a sincere appreciation of the bed as a place either for pleasurable activity or repose, and a recognition of the poetic role it plays in so many of the joys and sorrows of human life.

No work of this kind can be entirely original, and it is a pleasure to acknowledge the help we have received from many sources. All the books, articles, and papers from which we have drawn our facts are listed in the bibliography or bibliographical notes, and we must express our particular indebtedness to the writings of the late Reginald Reynolds, whose book *Beds* (1952) first drew our attention to the scope of the subject, and to the anthology called *The Bed* (1946) compiled by Cecil and Margery Gray, which introduced us to many amusing and apposite quotations. All students of the bed and bedroom activities are confidently referred to these works.

Our own book differs from its predecessors in three main respects. First, we have placed a rather greater emphasis on the scientific aspects of the subject, particularly the mechanism of sleep, as we believe that solid facts of this kind may be of at least equal interest with the more obviously entertaining sociological material. Second, we have included full documentation so that those who wish to follow up any particular aspect of the philosophy of the bed can go directly to the original sources without unnecessary labour. Third, and perhaps most important, we have placed a very strong emphasis on illustration. No previous contribution to the subject has been illustrated on such a scale and, whatever the shortcomings of the text, we are at least confident that the pictures of beds and their occupants as seen through the eyes of the world's great masters will be an acceptable recompense.

Acknowledgements are made to the following for the use of quotations from copyright works: Messrs. Chatto and Windus Ltd., for the quotations from *Sleep* by the late Dr. Marie Carmichael Stopes; the Hogarth Press, for extracts from *The Art of Dying* by Francis Birrell and F. L. Lucas; Messrs. Jonathan Cape Ltd., for the quotation from Edward MacCurdy's translation of *The Notebooks of Leonardo da Vinci;* the proprietors of *Time* for a quotation from the issue of January 14th, 1946; Messrs. Methuen and Co. Ltd., for the use of a translated passage from *Medieval People* by Eileen Power; Messrs. William Heinemann Ltd., for the quotation from *French Furniture under Louis XV* by Roger de Félice, and the translated passage from

14

the *Elegies* of Propertius; Beaverbrook Newspapers Ltd., for the quotation from *Sleep* by Chapman Pincher; Messrs. Geoffrey Bles Ltd., for the quotation from *The Arches of the Years* by Halliday Sutherland; the Falstaff Press, New York, for the translation of a French poem in *The Erotikon* by Augustin Cabanès; and the Trustees of the British Museum for the quotation from the booklet *Fleas* in their Economic Series.

Acknowledgements are also made to the following for the use of photographs and other illustrative material: Messrs. Thames and Hudson Ltd.; Dr. O. W. Sampson, Horniman Museum, London; Egyptian Museum, Cairo; Ashmolean Museum, Oxford; Accademia, Venice; Victoria and Albert Museum, London; Radio Times Hulton Picture Library; Oxford University Press, New York; Trustees of the British Museum; Ferdinand Enke Verlag, Stuttgart; Editor, *Practical Mechanics;* Collection V. W. Van Gogh, Laren; Louvre, Paris; Trustees of the National Gallery; National Gallery of Scotland, Edinburgh; Hermitage, Leningrad; Prado, Madrid; Kunsthistorisches Museum, Vienna; Nationalmuseum, Stockholm; Petit Palais, Paris; Collection Rodriguez-Henriques, Paris; Musée des Beaux Arts, Bordeaux; Collection de la Ville de Paris; Musée National d'Art Moderne, Paris; Musées Royaux des Beaux Arts, Antwerp; Associated Press Ltd.; Associated Newspapers Ltd.; Governors of Dulwich College, London; Editor, *The Sphere;* Colonel Reutlinger; Ministère de l'Information, Paris; Mathiesen Gallery, London; Mr. H. Tatlock Miller; and Mr. James Wentworth Day.

Finally our best thanks are due to Mr. John Hadfield for permission to use extracts from an article by Mary Eden which appeared in the 1958 issue of *The Saturday Book*.

MARY EDEN
RICHARD CARRINGTON

CHAPTER ONE

Of Beds and their Furnishings

THE first sleeping-place of primitive man was a pile of grass or brushwood in a simple hut or on the floor of a cave. A few living peoples have preserved this habit, and examples of beds of a very simple kind are known from many parts of the world. Thus sleeping naked in wood-ash is still practised by such primitive African tribes as the Dinka and the Nuer of the Nilotic Sudan, and is said to protect the sleeper from the attacks of insects. Among the Eskimoes and the inhabitants of Tierra del Fuego beds are made from piles of skins, which are also used as coverings to preserve warmth. In southern Asia it is often the custom to sleep on neatly woven mats, while in Polynesia the number and quality of bed-mats in a house are a sign of the wealth of the householder.[I]

Pillows and head-rests were also used by primitive man, and designs of great simplicity persist to this day. (See Plates 1 and 2.) The first pillow was simply a pile of straw, sometimes covered with a skin or woven cloth, and the simplest head-rest was nothing more sympathetic than a log of wood. But as man's artistic sense grew and found expression in decorating the articles and utensils found in his home, head-rests began to be less crudely fashioned. They were often carved in the form of animals, and were either coloured with vegetable dyes or decorated with pokerwork. The elaborate hair styles developed by primitive peoples encouraged the design of special head-rests to preserve the coiffure during sleep. Sometimes the head-rest was little more than a narrow bar mounted on two simple supports, but in some regions, notably Africa and South America, it evolved into a richly carved stool which was an object of great visual beauty.

By a bed today we normally mean a platform which is in some way raised several inches, or maybe as much as two or three feet, above the ground. The most primitive beds were at floor level, but the early stages in the evolution of true beds can be seen in such widely separated regions as the Sudan, West Africa, and the north-west coast of North America. Here it is the custom for benches of clay or soil to be built along the inner walls of huts and houses, and these are sometimes covered with comfortable plaited mattresses. Another primitive form of raised bed is the hammock, which probably originated either in New Guinea or South America. It has since found much favour with seamen, and in Victorian and Edwardian times offered a much appreciated means of taking an open-air siesta in the garden on a hot summer day. (See Plate 14a.) But we must remember that the hammock represents a side branch of the evolutionary line leading to the bed, and is not one of its direct ancestors.

With the growth of civilization, beds became increasingly elaborate in ornamentation and diverse in style. In ancient Egypt high bedsteads were particularly popular, and some models were reached by steps. These beds were surrounded by curtains, and were equipped with bolsters or pillows, and often half-cylinders of stone, wood, or metal as head-rests as well. Several beds were found among the treasure deposited in the tomb of the Eighteenth Dynasty boy pharaoh Tut-Ankh-Amen at Thebes. This was opened by Lord Carnarvon and Howard Carter in November 1922, and its contents are now exhibited in the Egyptian Museum at Cairo. Several beds were found in the tomb, the most perfect example being of carved ebony overlaid with sheet-gold. The legs were shaped like those of cats, and the decoration of the burnished gold foot-panel (the ancient Egyptians did not usually have head-panels to their beds) consisted of garlands of petals and fruits, bouquets, and clumps of papyrus and sedge. Another bed of less ornate design folded into three sections for travelling.[2] (See Plates 3a and b.)

The beds of the Assyrians, Medes, and Persians were similar to those of the ancient Egyptians, and were often beautifully ornamented with inlays of metal, mother of pearl, and ivory. The Persians especially were connoisseurs of the bed, and many classical writers speak of the emphasis they placed on luxurious sleeping arrangements. Thus we read in the eighth book of Xenophon's *Cyropaedia* how the Persian kings, not content with having the bed itself supremely soft and comfortable, insisted that it should be placed on a pile carpet to ensure a cushioning effect. Chares of Mytilene, a Greek belonging to the suite of Alexander the Great, records that the Persian kings demanded such refinements of luxury that their beds were canopied with golden vines inlaid with precious stones, while tables laden with gold and silver stood permanently adjacent to them.[3]

Compared with Persian and Egyptian beds, the earliest classical beds were simple. They consisted of a wooden frame, with a board at the head, and a latticework of cord or leather on which was laid a pile of skins. Later the beds became more elaborate, and were sometimes even made of solid ivory. Many examples were veneered with expensive woods or tortoise-shell, and both the Greeks and the Romans were addicted to rich bed-coverings and embroidered counterpanes. Some of their beds, like those of the ancient Egyptian, were so high that steps were needed to ascend to them.[4]

FIG. 1. *Solomon in bed. From Viollet-le-Duc (1855-8), Vol. 1, p. 173, after a MS. of Herrade de Landsberg in the Strasbourg Library*

The decline and fall of the Roman Empire was accompanied by the decline and fall of the bed throughout the whole of Europe. In England in Saxon times the beds were merely bags of straw, like the palliasses familiar to service-men in the last war, and the whole household often went to bed on the hall floor. In Germany in the Dark Ages the ancestors of Bismarck and Beethoven lay on the ground on piles of leaves, or in a kind of shallow chest filled with moss. Later they began to use mattresses stuffed with feathers, which they placed on a pile of carpets or on a bench by the wall. Here they used to sleep naked, wrapped in a linen sheet or covered with skins. The modern counterpart of these rather primitive and unsatisfactory arrangements is still to be found in Germany today, where too often a small square eiderdown, if it can be persuaded to stay on the bed at all, causes one end of the body to roast while the other is left to become stiff with cold.

The illuminated manuscripts of the early Middle Ages show that many medieval beds were still of fairly simple design. Nevertheless, a tendency towards greater ornateness and luxury can be detected as early as the twelfth century. Embroidered mattresses and coverings were designed to match the inlays, carvings, and paintings which decorated the bedstead itself. Curtains hung from the ceiling or from an iron arm projecting from the wall, which screened the slumberer from prying eyes, and the bed was usually shielded from draughts by being placed in a corner or recess. The upper part of the bed was covered with cushions, and many medieval pictures show its occupant reclining in a semi-sitting position. This seems to have been a common attitude of repose at the time, although it is certainly much exaggerated in some pictures by the draftsman's limited knowledge of the laws of perspective. (See Plates 13a and 49.)

A lamp was suspended over many medieval beds, just as nowadays most beds have a reading-lamp standing on a nearby table, or even fixed permanently to the headboard. The more academic historians of the bed have used up a great deal of paper in trying to explain why so many medieval beds were equipped in this way. Even an authority of the eminence of E. E. Viollet-le-Duc suggested that the bed-light was mainly necessary to reassure nervous persons who might fear the visitations of a ghost. Doubtless there is an element of truth in this, for the Middle Ages were notoriously superstitious; but no one seems to have considered that night fell at the same time in those days as it does now, and that medieval people may have appreciated a little illumination for their love-making (or even for writing, reading, and eating in bed) as much as we do.

Throughout the Middle Ages the bed showed a gradual increase in complexity, and the simple structures of earlier times were replaced by progressively more elaborate designs. Some models were surrounded by a kind of balustrade, with only a narrow opening at one side to provide an entrance and exit for the occupant. In the thirteenth century canopies were introduced, and during the next hundred years the decoration of the bed itself was subordinated to the increasingly sumptuous draperies by which it was enclosed. At

FIG. 2. *An Anglo-Saxon bed on wheels*

the same time there was a tendency for the bed to grow larger, and a length of seven or eight feet, with a width of six or seven feet, was by no means uncommon. Later, even larger beds were made, especially during the sixteenth and seventeenth centuries, and some of these will be described in a later chapter.

Thomas Fosbroke in his *Encyclopaedia of Antiquities*, published in 1825, gives some of the names of the different types of bedsteads used in classical times and the Middle Ages. Thus the *grabatum* was a low, portable bed used by Roman slaves and medieval rustics, the *archi-*

21

tectile was a wooden bedstead covered only with straw, and the *gyrgatus* was 'a bed used for lunaticks, when bound'. Another interesting bed was the *scympodium*; this consisted of a chair extended by a stool, and is said to be the bed referred to by Jesus when He said, 'Take up thy bed and walk.'[5]

The cult of the bed, which began in early Renaissance times, lasted until the growth of industrial society in the early nineteenth century, but thereafter, as we shall see, there was a new period of decline. Recently there has been a growing emphasis on simple comfort rather than the flamboyant styles that were formerly so popular. The resources of science and the skill of modern designers have brought a comfortable bed within the range of everyone's pocket, which is of course an excellent thing; but at the same time, rather sadly, the great English four-poster, with its magnificent carvings and draperies, has become a thing of the past. On the Continent, also, few can now afford the luxurious beds that once stood in every civilized home.

As we explained in the Preface, it is not our intention to discuss in detail the evolution of the bed as an article of furniture, but a brief description must be given of some aspects of its development in different ages and different regions.

In western Europe perhaps the finest beds were made in France, although some Italian Renaissance beds rivalled them in elegance. England, in keeping with the character of a northern and somewhat puritan nation, placed a greater emphasis on solidity, dignity, and magnitude in her beds than the more frivolous Continentals, who for some reason always seem to associate the bed primarily with sex. The Great Bed of Ware, and other majestic examples from England, are pre-eminently beds to be born and to die in, and the very thought of their being used for amorous dalliance, or indeed for any form of sensual activity (at least if it were enjoyed), seems almost blasphemous. Many French beds, on the other hand, are so seductively elegant and feminine in appearance that they seem fitted for little else, and one can almost imagine that for more serious activities, such as sickness and death, their owners must have been shipped across the Channel.

Between the beginning of the Renaissance and the French Revolution the various types of French beds were known by a bewildering variety of names. Thus there was the *lit d'ange*, without bed-posts but with canopy and side curtains; the *lit à l'anglaise*, resembling a high modern drawing-room sofa with a back and two end-pieces; the *lit à deux dossiers*, which was a *lit à l'anglaise* without a back; the *lit clos*, a bed enclosed by doors, which can still be seen in parts of Brittany; the *lit à colonnes*, the French four-poster; the *lit en tombeau*, a four-poster with the pillars higher at the head than the foot, with a sloping canopy; and the *lit de glace*, a characteristically French style of bed with mirrors at the sides or above. This by no means

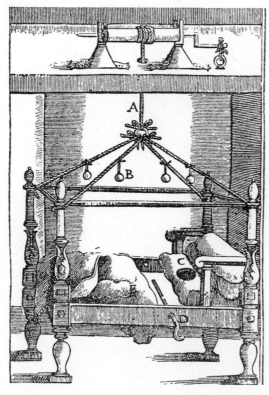

FIG. 3. *A French 'mechanical bed'. Its date of construction and its principles of operation are unknown*

exhausts the list, but a full recital of the different types would make tedious reading for the non-specialist. Those interested in the subject are referred to the third volume of Henry Havard's *Dictionnaire de l'Ameublement et de la Décoration* (1887—90), where sixty-nine types of French bed are fully described.

The rulers of France always paid great attention to their beds, and the draperies of many royal bedsteads were extremely sumptuous. For instance, the great bed at Versailles had its crimson velvet

23

curtains so heavily embroidered that the velvet scarcely showed. The embroidery at first depicted *The Triumph of Venus*, a subject in which Louis XIV took especial delight; but under the influence of the religious Marquise de Maintenon, who was at first his mistress but married him after the death of Marie Thérèse, a new set was ordered showing *The Sacrifice of Abraham*. Fortunately the king had a number of alternative resting-places if he so desired, for the inventories of his palaces show that he possessed no fewer than four hundred and thirteen beds.

In England the curtained and canopied four-poster was the usual bed of the wealthy citizen until the middle of the mineteenth century. This type of bed reached its highest development in Tudor and Stuart times, when bedsteads were less articles of furniture than pieces of architecture. Oak was the wood most commonly employed, although we know that Queen Elizabeth I, when not trying out the beds up and down the country where she is alleged to have slept, sometimes used a bedstead of richly carved walnut with draperies of cloth of silver. Many examples of such magnificent structures can still be seen in old country houses, and some have also found their way into museums. Few things are more depressing than to see such a living object as a bed in a museum, but it must be admitted that the idea of actually sleeping on a Tudor four-poster is rather forbidding.

In the eighteenth century English beds became smaller and less architectural in style. Mahogany largely replaced oak, and was a favourite wood with such well-known furniture designers as Chippendale, Sheraton, and Hepplewhite. These masters retained the essence of the four-poster style, but turned it into a less awe-inspiring structure which could be used with positive enjoyment. They managed to achieve something of the elegant spirit of the French bed without too ruthless a violation of the English tradition.

The Italian contribution to the history of the bed has been quite outshone by the French, but individual Italian beds are of great beauty, and our subject would be much poorer without them. The characteristic Italian style was developed in the early part of the fifteenth century and, in spite of the French invasion, persisted for some two hundred years. The Venetian bed is the best-known type and was an object of great dignity and luxury. It stood upon a dais, or *predella*, and the canopy, often of fantastic shape, was supported by four slender columns. The wooden panels at the head and foot were elaborately carved and painted, and the furnishings included feather mattresses, fine linen sheets, and silken counterpanes. The canopy, which supported thick velvet curtains, was itself highly ornamented with biblical scenes, or perhaps with a representation of the star-studded sky.

By the beginning of the nineteenth century in all parts of western Europe the bed had gone into a new decline. Victorian beds were as heavy and uninspiring as the other furniture of the period, while

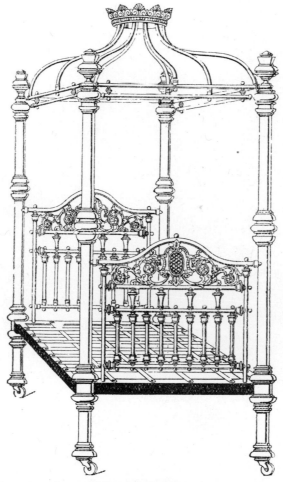

FIG. 4. *A gracefully designed four-poster in brass taken from a current catalogue. Brass bedsteads are still very much in demand, particularly in Africa*

25

on the Continent there was often an undue emphasis on extravagant and bizarre ornamentation. For example, the Austrian statesman Metternich tells us in his *Memoirs* of two extraordinary beds which were installed in the palace of Furstenberg in 1820. They resembled draped rockeries, and were ornamented with bats and toads of gilded wood and carved lizards as big as a man's hand. The beds stood in an alcove lighted by a lamp in the form of an owl, two beams of light issuing from its eyes. These extraordinary beds, we are told, cost forty thousand florins apiece.[6]

The typical modern bed, consisting usually of a box spring, with or without head- and foot-panels, and supported by short legs, may have reached perfection in terms of comfort, but no one could call it inspiring in appearance. We must therefore be grateful to such designers and interior decorators as Eszter Haraszty, John Loper, Guy Roop, and others who have pioneered a new conception of the bed which is thouroughly in keeping with the spirit of contemporary life. Their various attractive designs for divans and canopied four-posters in modern light-weight metals and decorated in the idiom of our times show that not everything produced in the second half of the twentieth century is either reactionary or ugly.

Although America has set a very high standard in modern bed designs, Britain can also show a much wider range of adventurous models than was available before the war, or even in the early ninetcen-fifties. Many of the new British-designed beds are extremely elegant, and fit well into the general styling of the contemporary home. Among curiosities, perhaps the most remarkable bed ever to have been made was the British model shown at the Furniture Exhibition at Earls Court in 1959, and described in the *Daily Express* for January 15th of that year under the heading: 'The Electronic Road to Ritzy Relaxation'. The bed was for two people, but instead of a double mattress it had two single ones three feet wide. These could be separately adjusted to any position at the touch of a button, and individually heated to the required temperature, which was then automatically maintained. At either side of the bed-head was a built-in unit providing for the two sleepers' every want. The man's unit was equipped with a telephone, an electric shaver, and a tape-recorder for business dictation; the woman's with an automatic tea-maker, a silver tea-service, and an electric massage machine. Each unit had an individual radio, which perhaps compensated slightly for the presence of only a single television set attached to the foot of the bed. A switch-board within reach of both occupants controlled the bedroom lights and the television, and opened or closed the bedroom curtains. The bed could be wired up to every other room in the house by an inter-communication system. Strangely enough, the sheets and blankets were of conventional type, but mink coverlets reassured the owner that his bed was after all rather better than the Jones's. The cost of this 'machine for living', as the *Daily Express* called it, was £2,500, and if it can scarcely be expected to find its way into many bed-rooms at the present stage of our economic development it at least forms a fitting climax —or anticlimax —to our account of the Western bed as an article of furniture. (See Plate 15*b*.)

Let us now turn, with something like relief, to a few examples from other regions. Many ancient travellers remarked on the nature of the beds in the countries they visited. For instance, Marco Polo, as translated by Colonel Yule, describes a type of bed used by 'nobles and great folks' in the province of Maabar in southern India. He writes:

> 'The men of this country have their beds made of very light canework, so arranged that, when they have got in and are going to sleep, they are drawn up by cords nearly to the ceiling and fixed there for the night. This is done to get out of the way of tarantulas which give terrible bites, as well as of fleas and such vermin, and at the same time to get as much air as possible in the great heat which prevails in that region.'[7]

William Marsden, another translator of Marco Polo, renders the passage differently, saying that the beds were not hauled up to the ceiling, but that insect-proof curtains could be drawn round them by a string. Yule will have none of this translation, but whatever the rights and wrongs of the matter, it is certainly a fact that beds with built-in mosquito-nets of this kind, but rather more elaborate in structure, were known in the Ming period in China (1368 – 1644). These were normally placed against the rear wall of a small square room, being approached through an ante-room separated from the bedchamber by sliding doors. They were simply covered with matting, and were thus never so luxurious as some of the beds known

27

at this time in the Near and Middle East. These consisted of a low rostrum, covered to a great depth with numbers of soft cushions. The sleeper reclined on these in voluptuous ease, clad in some soft garment, but unencumbered by sheets, blankets, or other coverings.

The mats used for sleeping in India have already been referred to (page 17), but there is also a primitive bedstead in common use there known as the *charpoy*. This consists of a simple framework of wood supporting a lattice of interwoven ropes. It is extremely comfortable, and sufficiently portable to be moved into a courtyard, or even into the street, at night so that the sleeper can have the benefit of the cool air. But the educated Indian is inclined to despise the *charpoy*, and prefers to sleep on a bed of Western type, usually elaborately designed to his own specifications and exported from London or Paris. (See Plate 14*b*). The only other bed of any note to be found in India consists of a board covered with rows of upward-pointing nails; but this is reserved for fakirs, and less ascetic members of the community do not regard it with enthusiasm. (See Plate 16*b*.)

The last nation we shall have space to mention here is Japan which is remarkable less for the variety or intrinsic interest of her bedsteads than for the fact that until recently she had no bedsteads at all. Even today the majority of Japanese sleep between two simple quilts—the *shiki-futon*, or under-quilt, and the *kake-futon*, or over-quilt. By day the quilts are put away in a closet, but at night they are unrolled on a mat, known as a *tatami*, which covers the whole floor of the room. In cold weather the room is warmed by a device known as a *kotatsu*, which consists of a wooden box containing a charcoal-burner. This is placed in the middle of the *tatami*, and whole families may sleep around it, their feet pointing to the *kotatsu* and their bodies radiating outwards like the spokes of a wheel.

So much, then, for beds themselves, ancient and modern, simple, sophisticated, and bizarre; now what of bedding?

To begin with the mattress, the physical basis of all the bed's accoutrements, we can quote in the first instance no less an authority than the late Dr. Marie Carmichael Stopes, the eminent palaeobotanist and authority on birth-control.

In her book *Sleep* she writes:

'The finest, springiest and most comfortable mattress in the world is dry summer heather. It needs but a curtain of bracken

28

above one's head to prevent excessive radiation from oneself up to the sky, and a sight of bright stars between the bracken fronds to enthrone one on a bed fit for the gods.'[8]

But as Dr. Stopes herself observes, 'such a mattress cannot be commended for every night use, even by the fortunate, for it may rain heavily'. What, then, are the practical alternatives?

As we have seen, leaves and straw have been used by man to sleep on from the very earliest times, but civilized nations (by which, of course, we mean those which have succeeded in releasing into the atmosphere a respectable quantity of Strontium 90) are inclined to frown on such primitive foundations for the bed. For these the mattress stuffed with fearthers has for long been the most popular, although it is by no means the best for health, being liable to inflame certain allergies. As long ago as the fifteenth century Leonardo da Vinci was prophesying, while deploring the prospect, the widespread use of the feather mattress. 'There will be a great host,' he wrote in his *Notebooks*, 'who, forgetful of their existence and their name, will lie as though dead upon the spoils of other dead creatures: by sleeping upon the feathers of birds.'[9]

But in Leonardo had taken his dislike of soft mattresses too far, he would quickly have found himself confronting the formidable Dr. Stopes. 'A *soft* mattress is my choice,' she writes; 'hard mattresses are often advised for hygienic reasons, but this seems to me wrong. . . . A soft mattress is one of the good things we can now readily obtain.' Nevertheless Dr. Stopes was violently opposed to the soft foam-rubber mattress which is now tending to replace the traditional feather-bed of the past. In fact for one who made so many valuable contributions to the science of contraception she seems to have had a surprisingly uncompromising attitude towards some of the other uses for rubber. She writes:

'The soft foam-rubber mattress is an example of a modern "advance" to be avoided by all who value their health. It is pernicious. Do *not* use any rubber mattress, and do *not* have rubber-tyred wheels upon your bedstead. Why? Because rubber is an insulator, and cuts you off from electric currents of the earth with which you should be in contact. Many, sadly many, people are insulating themselves incessantly. Rubber-soled shoes

29

all day, and then rubber covering to their floors, small wheels with rubber tyres on their beds—alas, poor things, they are being devitalized. No wonder millions at the end of the day feel limp and exhausted....'[10]

Mattresses, you will see, are a depressing theme. Let us therefore turn more hopefully to bolsters and pillows. Fosbroke tells us that in Roman times there was no distinction between the bolster and the pillow, and the Roman pillow, 'at least for ladies', was stuffed with the finest down. The ancient Saxon pillow was very stiff and hard, and the bolster was sometimes made of plaited straw. It was once customary for every bed to be equipped with a pile of at least three pillows of different sizes, the smallest being placed on top.[11] The custom of having numerous pillows has already been noted as characteristic of the Near and Middle East, but is not limited to those regions. The late Enrico Caruso, one of the finest tenors of all time, was accustomed to sleep with up to eighteen pillows, as well as three mattresses.[12] This may seem something of an exaggeration, but the pillow is certainly one of the major achievements of civilization, as anyone who has tried a native head-rest, or even a tin hat or gas-mask case in wartime, will realize. Dr. Stopes, let it be added, was strongly in favour of pillows, and insisted that for civilized people they should be as soft as possible. 'I have used large flat stones as pillows when touring,' she writes, 'but they numb one's nerves, and are not to be recommended.'[13]

The coverings of the bed need not be considered at length, although it is noteworthy that the modern arrangement of sheets and blankets came into use at a very early date. In classical times the poorer people had to be content with a simple covering, such as a sheep-skin with the wool on it, but the Roman patricians obtained fine white linen from Gaul. The Anglo-Saxons used both sheets and blankets. The most primitive Saxon blanket was simply a bear- or goat-skin, but others were woven, either of fustian or, more rarely, of high-quality wool. The Anglo-Saxon sheets were known as *sceta*, and in the richer homes were often made of linen and embroidered with precious stones. On the Continent in the fourteenth and fifteenth centuries noble ladies were accustomed to use sheets of black satin in place of the more usual white, in the belief that by showing up the pallor of their skins they would become still more alluring to their lovers. At that time the whiteness of the skin was considered one of the main criteria of a woman's attractiveness, and black sheets maintained their popularity among courtesans and other disciples of Eros for many centuries. Only in the last thirty or forty years has the cult of sun-tan reduced the effectiveness of this particular aid to allure.

Much more could be written about other furnishings of the bed, such as quilts, counterpanes, eiderdowns, and embroidered draperies, but the subject is too vast to be covered in a small book of this kind. Moreover we have promised that our account of beds shall be more concerned with the role they have played in human life than with their physical nature and trappings. In the next chapter, therefore, we shall pass on from the solid material object we know as a bed to its relationship with the men and women who are accustomed to inhabit it.

CHAPTER TWO

Some Aspects of Bedroom Life

BEDS have always caused strong emotions in the human heart, and in all ages and among all peoples they have become the subject of many strange superstitions. For instance among the Mende of Sierra Leone if a man sits on the bed of his mother or his sister it is regarded as equivalent to incest,[14] while a common superstition among simple people even in so-called civilized societies is that the young lose their vitality by sharing a bed with the old.[15] According to Wilhelm Bleek, when the Bushmen of South Africa go hunting any failure to shoot down the quarry is attributed to the fact that the children at home are playing on the hunter's bed; quite rightly, the wife is held responsible for this lapse of parental control and duly scolded for it when the men return.[16]

Illicit goings on in the bed during the absence of a hunter are regarded as a source of grave misfortune to him. We can learn from the great anthropologist Sir James Frazer in *The Golden Bough* that if in the latter years of the last century an inhabitant of the Aleutians failed to kill a sea-otter this was attributed to the fact that his wife had been unfaithful to him, or his sister unchaste.[17] Similarly, the Moxos Indians of eastern Bolivia believed that if a hunter's wife took another man into her bed during his absence he would assuredly be bitten by a serpent or mauled by a jaguar. If such a misfortune befell him the logic of his simple mind dictated that the wife should be severely punished, or even put to death, whether she was guilty of the act or not.[18] One of the present authors has recorded some related customs found among the elephant hunters of West Africa. These relate to the Mundassas of Gabon and the Middle Congo, who consider it auspicious for the *Njanga djoko*, or master of the elephant rite, to take his wife to bed for sexual intercourse on the eve of the hunt. Rather unfairly, the rank and file of the huntsmen are forbidden this pleasurable start to their adventure, although they are allowed to indulge themselves as soon as the hunt has been successfully concluded.[19]

Magical beliefs are not restricted to the bed itself, but in some regions are also associated with the bedclothes. A particularly notable instance, which probably originated among the primitive inhabitants of eastern Europe, seems to have survived even into the rational times of ancient Greece. Frazer reminds us that the disciples of Pythagoras insisted that the impression left by the body in the bedclothes should always be smoothed away on rising. He claims that this superstition was an example of 'contagious magic', which is still found among primitive tribes today. Thus the aborigines of south-eastern Australia believe that a man may be injured by stabbing the mark left by his reclining body with sharp fragments of quartz. Likewise the natives of Tumleo, an island off New Guinea, always smooth over the spot where they have lain as a protection against witchcraft.[20]

But we should not think that superstitions concerning the bed are restricted to ancient times or primitive people. As recently as the sixteenth century King Henry VII of England, in defiance of rheumatism, had his bed sprinkled every night with holy water to ward off evil spirits, while even today it is still commonly believed that sleep is difficult or impossible if the bed is not orientated along the north-south axis of the earth. Charles Dickens was one of those who subscribed to this view, and a boy with a 'sense of the north' is a character in Du Maurier's *Peter Ibbetson*. But this splendid piece of magic has survived even in scientific circles. Dr. Stopes, for example, always insisted on the correct orientation of the bed, although she regarded it as comparatively unimportant whether the head or the feet were at the north end. When she visited a house where her bed happened to be out of alignment she could not sleep until she had moved it to the north and south direction. If it was too heavy for her she would lie across it slantwise in the most determined manner, even though this made the bedclothes 'rather uncomfortable'. Perhaps her most remarkable achievement in the field of orientation was actually to locate the source of the 'sense of the north' in her own body.

'It is in my spine that I magnetate the north,' she wrote, 'between my shoulder-blades and hips. I used to have this sense so intensely that I could be blindfolded in a fog on a desolate moor and twisted round a great number of times, and could at once point to the exact north. This was tested by geologists with a compass....'[21]

Being now forewarned of some of the possible hazards of bedroom life, the time has come to make our first intrepid advance upon the bed itself. In warm weather the actual plunge between the sheets is a pleasing and relaxing experience, but in winter it can be almost as disagreeable as taking a cold bath. For civilized people, therefore, one of the main necessities of bedroom life is to devise some means of warming the bed before getting into it. The most obvious way is, of course, to ensure that one's partner is there before one to take the first chill off the sheets; but this inevitably leads to accusations of unfairness, and offers no solution to those who by necessity or preference habitually sleep alone. Fortunately the products of scientific invention and human ingenuity have now made it possible for the problem to be solved in various effective ways. The warming-pan was one of the earliest and most obvious, and was extremely satisfactory in the days when an open fire burned in every hearth. Heated bricks and smoothing-irons wrapped in flannel, devices of more recent introduction, also gave a certain amount of comfort. Among more unusual methods, Reynolds records an instance where a friend of his in Newfoundland had his bed warmed for him by the simple expedient of a baby being placed in it first.[22] Today the field is almost equally divided between devotees of the hot-water bottle and the electric blanket. The latter, although a scientifically sound invention, still has about it a suggestion of danger, if not of immorality. But those who hesitate to avail themselves of this method of warming the bed may be encouraged to learn that hot-water bottles themselves were equally feared and despised when first introduced in the early years of the nineteenth century. There is perhaps little to choose between the dangers of being scalded or electrocuted when one is really in need of a good night's sleep.

Dr. Stopes was particularly suspicious of hot-water bottles, especially the gay, coloured variety that replaced the 'pure dull grey rubber that bottles were made of before and during the last war'. After having acquired one of these frivolous and licentious objects she suddenly began to experience nagging and painful cramp in her legs and feet. 'This kind of affliction seemed to be rather common at that time,' she wrote, 'for I saw several mentions of it in the medical papers as "one of the sufferings brought by the passing years".' Her reaction was characteristic: 'Rot! It was brought, as I fortunately discovered for myself, by the stink given off by my new rubber hot-water bottle.'[23]

Having decided on the best method of warming the bed, the next matter that must be weighed in the balance is whether or not the same bed may be legitimately shared by two persons. Double beds were known to the Greeks and Romans, and communal sleeping is practised by races as divergent in philosophy as the Eskimoes and the Japanese. But in Paris, New York, and London, as well as other centres of Western civilization, the problem has subtle ramifications that cannot be simply dismissed by an appeal to historical or anthropological precedents. In the first-named city, of course, and in fact throughout France, the double bed is the rule, and the British demand for a *chambre à deux lits* is regarded as a charming but incomprehensible foible of the eccentric foreigner. Among English-speaking peoples, however, the exact opposite is the case, and numerous authorities have spoken out strongly in favour of separate beds, or even separate rooms, for man and woman.

One of the most eloquent crusaders against the double bed was a certain Dr. James Graham, who practised in London in the late eighteenth century. We shall meet him again later in connection with one of the most notable beds ever devised by man, but in the meantime let him be the spokesman of the anti-double-bed school of thought:

'Gentlemen, there is not, in my opinion, anything in nature which is more immediately calculated totally to subvert health, strength, love, esteem, and indeed every thing that is desirable in the married state, than that odious, most indelicate, and most hurtful custom of man and wife continually *pigging* together, in one and the same bed. Nothing is more unwise—nothing more indecent—nothing more unnatural, than for a man and woman to sleep, and snore, and steam, and do every thing else that's indelicate together, three hundred and sixty-five times—every year.'[24]

Whether one shares one's bed or not, a matter that must be decided at an early stage is what, if anything, one should wear when one gets into it. Although Reynolds quotes a young South African lady who broke off her engagement when she learnt that her fiancé actually took his clothes off when he went to bed,[25] the custom of disrobing, or at least changing into some other costume, has become conventional. A glamorous actress has been quoted as saying that she prefers to sleep in nothing but a dab of Chanel No. 5 behind each ear, and nakedness has much to recommend it. To sleep naked was a common practice in the Middle Ages, as is proved by reference to contemporary documents. For example, C. Willett Cunnington quotes a fourteenth-century romance where a man is described as going to bed wearing both his shirt and drawers; this was obviously

FIG. 5. *Lady on a camp bed. From Havard (1887—90), Vol. 3, col. 422, after a miniature in MS. 2193 in the Bibliothèque de l'Arsenal, Paris*

regarded as a most unusual eccentricity. Further evidence comes from the same source in instructions to young women on going to bed; the last to undress was enjoined to snuff out the candle with her finger and thumb and not 'by throwing her chemise at it'. This certainly suggests that she did not intend to pause and put on a nightdress.[26] Finally a further proof is to be found, by implication, in the bed laws of Bishop Hugo Gratianopolitanus which clearly insist that monks, while removing their boots at night, must continue to wear their habits and socks. If nakedness had not been the custom in lay circles these injunctions would scarcely have been necessary.

Medieval illustrations nevertheless show that night-clothes were worn in certain circumstances, such as for 'lying-in' and during ceremonial visits. By Tudor times they had much increased in popularity, especially among the well-to-do, and wrought night-shirts are included in the wardrobe accounts of Henry VIII. At the beginning of the sixteenth century girls wore smocks in bed, which seem on occasion to have been rather unmanageable garments, as is shown by the following extract from John Aubrey's *Brief Lives*. Aubrey is describing the manner in which Sir William Roper selected one of the daughters of Sir Thomas More to be his wife. After reminding the reader that More had decreed in his famous *Utopia* (1516) that young people should see each other stark naked before marriage, Aubrey continues:

'Sir William Roper of Eltham in Kent, came one morning, pretty early, to my Lord, with a proposall to marry one of his daughters. My Lord's daughters were then both together abed in a truckle-bed in their father's chamber asleep. He carries Sir William into the chamber and takes the Sheete by the corner and suddenly whippes it off. They lay on their Backs, and their smocks up as high as their arme-pitts. This awakened them, and immediately they turned on their bellies. Quoth Roper, I have seen both sides, and so gave a patt on the buttock, he made choice of, sayeing, Thou art mine. Here was all the trouble of the wooeing.' [27]

In seventeenth-century England the male night-shirt was a most elaborate garment, often with lace insertions in the neck and sleeves, and ruffles at the wrist. A century later in Italy glamorous night-shirts of this type were worn at informal gatherings on hot evenings, where they were pleasingly referred to as *vestimenti di confidenza*. The cult of the night-shirt was so advanced at this time that black night-shirts and black night-caps were worn by gentlemen in mourning.

The evolution of the male night-shirt can be studied at the Victoria and Albert Museum (where there is, incidentally, an appealing example which belonged to Mr. Thomas Coutts, the famous banker). In the late nineteenth century the garment went into a decline, and was replaced by the familiar pyjamas which have remained in vogue ever since. For fifty years these were manufactured almost exclusively in broad coloured stripes which reduced men's sexual attractiveness in the bedroom to that of multi-coloured zebras. There is now merci-fully a trend towards plainer and more distinguished designs, and many members of the younger generation have abandoned wearing pyjamas altogether.

Except in the agreeable sense of a late evening whisky, the night-cap went out of vogue at the same time as the night-shirt. This marked the end of a glorious career which had lasted well over four hundred years. The richer connoisseurs of bedroom life often pos-sessed several dozen night-caps, most of them richly embroidered. Red was a favourite colour, perhaps to suggest warmth, and Cun-nington quotes two early suggestions for the materials and design. One is from a Dr. Andrew Borde, who wrote in 1557: 'Let your nyght cap ... be made of a good thycke quylte of cotton, or els of pure flockes or of cleane wolle.' The other, from William Vaughan, is dated 1602 and makes a point that no one seems previously to have thought of: 'Let your night cappe have a hole in the top through which the vapour may goe out.'[28]

Most of the evidence concerning women's night-clothes in the past comes from painting. Unfortunately we do not know the design of the smocks which led to the discomfiture of More's daughters, but in the next century the upper classes had their night-dresses richly trimmed with lace. Thereafter the garment changed little until Victoria's reign, when mass-produced night attire began to replace the bespoke or home-made articles of earlier times. In 1849 night-dresses were advertised for as little as 29*s*. 6*d*. a dozen, although a richly trimmed model might cost 7*s*. 6*d*. There was no great demand for these, however, as trimmings were regarded as likely to stimulate carnal thoughts in the opposite sex, and must therefore be an invention of the devil. Strangely the birth-rate failed to show any marked decline as a result of this attitude, and the transparent and seductive night-dresses of today suggest that women have learnt to accept the inevitable where men are concerned, and if possible to enjoy it.

We will allow the last word on night attire to Dr. Stopes, who was as eloquent on this subject as on every other aspect of bedroom life. She did not approve of pyjamas, which she regarded as the most uncomfortable sleeping garment ever devised. 'If there is a cord it catches and girds, the waist parts generally divide, and a chill rakes the middle.' She suggested that pyjamas should be made in one piece, like combinations, 'for grown-up men by tailors'. Even so she did not care for them herself, preferring night-dresses of real silk, sleeveless with a lace top, and so long that they would trail for about eight inches on the ground in the vertical position. 'In this length,' she wrote, 'the feet are enclosed when lying down so there are no horrid draughts anywhere.' Moreover the only thing good enough for the author of *Married Love* was 'good, real, exquisitely soft Oriental silk'. There was never any question that she could ever be fobbed off with artificial silk or any of those nasty new-fangled materials made from chemicals.

'What *rubbish* we women are served with nowadays!' she ex-claims indignantly. 'It is iniquitous that cellulose fabrications should be allowed to call themselves "pure silk" and so deceive women into thinking they are getting silk when they are not. The only pure silk in the world is made by silk-worms and gives indescribable comfort undreamed of by the wearers of "silk" and nylon. Real silk-worm silk is a delicate web for the capture of sleep.'[29]

Leaving Dr. Stopes thus happily wrapped in her cocoon, we turn next to the delicate question of whom, if anyone, the bed should be shared with. There are strong arguments, as we have seen, for isolation in this respect, but neither of the present authors is able to accept them without reserve. The horrors of the double bed at its worst have been graphically summarized by Dr. Graham in the passage already quoted, but we should remember that it is by no means necessary for the experience of spending the night *à deux* to be as revolting as this. Certainly no young lover should be discouraged from sleeping alongside the person closest to his heart by views as one-sided as Dr. Graham's. If at a later stage either member of the partnership shows an excessive tendency to 'snore and steam', then the sleeping arrangements can always be changed.

While on the subject of sharing beds, a few unusual instances from the past should be noted. It might be thought that a man normally goes to bed with a woman for purposes of pleasure, or at least the anticipation of pleasure, but this was far from true in the early days of the Christian Church. Reynolds quotes numerous instances of the saints and martyrs sharing the bed of some glamorous siren for the express purpose of self-mortification. St. Aldhelm of Malmesbury took the matter even further, and habitually spent his nights with a girl lying on either side of him. By some logic difficult to understand in the mid-twentieth century, this practice was supposed to be for his moral good—not, let it be said at once, for the opportunities it gave for healthful exercise and relaxation, but because it showed his powers of resistance to the temptations of the devil. An even more astonishing reason, regarded as equally important, was that people would be certain to misconstrue his actions and therefore to speak ill of him; such a supreme refinement of self-torture was thought at the time to be a particularly valid contribution towards a passport to heaven.

Gibbon has an interesting passage concerning this odd form of self-mortification in the fifteenth chapter of the *Decline and Fall*. He writes:

'The chaste severity of the fathers, in whatever related to the commerce of the two sexes, flowed from the same principle: their abhorrence of every enjoyment which might gratify the sensual, and degrade the spiritual, nature of man. It was their favourite opinion that, if Adam had preserved his obedience to the Creator, he would have lived for ever in a state of virgin purity, and that some harmless mode of vegetation might have peopled paradise with a race of innocent and immortal beings.... The primitive church was filled with a great number of persons of either sex who had devoted themselves to the profession of perpetual chastity.... Some were insensible and some were invincible against the assaults of the flesh. Disdaining an ignominious flight, the virgins of the warm climate of Africa encountered the enemy in the closest engagement; they permitted priests and deacons to share their bed, and gloried amidst the flames in their unsullied purity. But insulted Nature sometimes vindicated her rights, and this new species of martyrdom served only to introduce a new scandal into the church.'[30]

But pleasure or asceticism are not the only reasons for sharing beds; sometimes the cause has simply been poverty or lack of space. Instances of whole families sleeping in one bed were common as recently as twenty years ago, and still occur, although fortunately to a much lesser extent, under the welfare state. All of us have probably shared a bed from necessity rather than choice in wartime and other emergencies, such as when careless guests have missed the last train home. A notable example of such an impromptu sharing of beds occurs in Chapter 31 of Herman Melville's *Moby Dick*, where the narrator Ishmael was reluctantly compelled to sleep with Queequeg, the cannibal harpooneer; but this, of course, is fiction. More authentic, but no less strange, examples are known from history, and sometimes an invitation to share the bed was regarded as a high mark of favour not necessarily connected with sexuality. Thus after Charles VIII of France was reconciled to the Duc d'Orleans he habitually shared his couch with him, and François I used to invite Admiral Bonnivet into his bed as a gesture of special esteem.[31]

Having warmed the bed, and decided whether to sleep in company or alone, the next thing is simply to turn down the sheets and get into it. Yet 'simply' is perhaps the wrong word, for even this apparently straightforward operation can be performed in an unusual way. Readers of Mrs. Gaskell's *Cranford* will recall how the elderly Miss Matty brought herself to confess that

'ever since she had been a girl, she had dreaded being caught by her last leg, just as she was getting into bed, by some one concealed under it. She said, when she was younger and more active, she used to take a flying leap from a distance, and so bring both her legs safely up into bed at once.... It was very unpleasant to think of looking under a bed, and seeing a man concealed, with a great fierce face staring out at you.'

41

Unfortunately Miss Matty's advancing years had eventually made this method of getting into bed too athletic, so she had obtained instead

'a penny ball, such as children play with—and now she rolled this ball under the bed every night; if it came out on the other side, well and good; if not, she always took care to have her hand on the bell-rope, and meant to call out "John" and "Harry", just as if she expected men-servants to answer her ring'.[32]

It should not be thought that such precautions against sinister persons lurking in the bedroom are necessarily confined to the pages of fiction. One of the present authors had a nurse in childhood who habitually made wild lunges under the bed with a broomstick before retiring in case of possible 'burglars'. Why a burglar should have been skulking in such an unlikely situation, or what she would have done with him if he had been, were questions it would have been imprudent to ask.

Difficult, and indeed dangerous, as it can sometimes be to get into bed, some people find that the act of getting out of it again poses still greater problems. Dr. Johnson used to lie in bed till noon or even later, but was always impressed by those who resisted such temptations. His preoccupation with the problem of early rising is shown in his approving report to Boswell concerning a certain Mrs. Carter who, he said, 'at that period when she was eager in study, did not awake as early as she wished, and she therefore had a contrivance, that, at a certain hour, her chamber-light should burn a string to which a heavy weight was suspended, which then fell with a strong sudden noise'.[33] The great naturalist Buffon was likewise obsessed with the idea that he should rise early to pursue his studies; but he had so little confidence in his ability to do so that he instructed his man-servant that if necessary he was to be ejected from his bed by force.[34] For some reason to lie in bed late in the morning is still regarded as lazy, and even immoral, so the reader may be particularly glad to learn that this view is scientifically quite unsound. It will be considered more fully, and we hope convincingly demolished, in a later chapter. (See Chapter 6.)

Making the bed after leaving it is one of the most tedious aspects of bedroom life, and research has revealed that a housewife with three beds to make can walk upwards of a dozen miles and spend about seventy-five hours each year at this single occupation.[35] Bed-making in certain circumstances can even be a danger to society, and the following gem, to which Reginald Reynolds sent us in the pages of *Time* magazine, shows the kind of hazard one may be exposed to at the hands of a really determined practitioner of the art:

'WOMANPOWER. In Chicago, Mrs. Alberta Brooks accidentally dropped a bed on a car parked beneath her window, explained: "When I shake my bedding, I shake it bed and all. It just slipped out of my hands." '[36]

Apart from its familiar uses the bed can fulfil a number of less obvious functions. In the first place it can, of course, be eaten in, and the Greeks and Romans so much enjoyed eating in the horizontal position that they took their main meals each day recumbent on a couch. Another traditional use for the bed is in the punishment of children, although many adults will find it difficult to remember a time when to be sent to bed was more of a penalty than a reward. Certainly we must doubt the efficacy of the mysterious threat in *Revelations* ii. 22 to throw Jezebel into a bed; just the kind of place she would have felt at home in, one would have thought. More unusually, the bed has occasionally served as a protection against thunderbolts. According to the Grays, Saint-Simon knew a lady who took refuge beneath her bed whenever there was a thunderstorm, and to make assurance doubly sure instructed all her servants to lie on top of it.[37] As a means of locomotion beds have obvious drawbacks, despite the fact that Cardinal Richelieu liked to be carried about in one. A much more satisfactory use for them, as some theatrical producers have discovered, is in the casting of plays. To conclude we must not forget Plato's great dialogue in the *Republic*, where the bed is discussed as an idea in the mind of God; nor, at the other extreme, the pathetic but useful end of so many derelict bedsteads as makeshift fencing round allotments.

Such examples will perhaps be sufficient to show the immense range of uses to which the bed can be put. So far, however, we have had but little to say concerning the bed's more fundamental role in the physical and spiritual evolution of man. We shall turn next to the first great adventure in our lives which normally occurs in bed: the act of being born.

43

CHAPTER THREE

Birth

BIRTH, like death, is one of the most mysterious and awe-inspiring events in the experience of man, and in consequence it has been the cause of many strange beliefs and superstitions. Probably because the pains of labour are so evident, and because delivery sometimes leads to the death of the mother, primitive peoples tend to picture birth as being presided over by a number of warring forces. Benevolent gods offer help and relief from pain, while demons are hostile and obstructive.

Most primitive people are not, of course, born in any kind of bed that we would recognize as such; they must make do with a blanket on the floor of a hut, a pile of straw, or some other equally simple

FIG. 6. *The birth of Brahma, after an Indian painting. From Witkowski (1887), p. 3*

arrangement. In some cases, owing to the primitive belief that parturition is unclean, they are banished from their homes and bring forth their children in the open air. More civilized societies allow their women to bear children in the comparative comfort of a bed at home, but the customs connected with the practice have varied through the ages. Greek women, for example, were normally confined in their own bedrooms, whereas Roman women retired to a room specially set apart for the purpose. The Roman woman would then wash, bind her head, and lie down on her couch, which was hung with rich draperies. The room itself was equipped with various objects that would be needed for the birth, including warm water, soft sponges, cotton binders, perfumes, a delivery chair, and two beds.[38]

Apart from enforced segregation due to the supposed uncleanliness of parturition, the woman has herself a natural instinct to withdraw at such times. Among the poorer classes, even in quite civilized

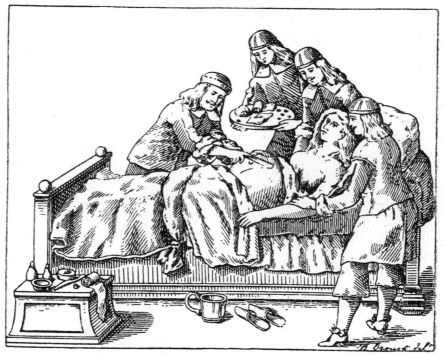

FIG. 7. *A Caesarean operation in the eighteenth century. From Witkowski (1887), p. 269, after Jean Scultet (1712)*

communities, the privacy required by the expectant mother is often difficult to obtain. Primitive peoples do at least sometimes provide a 'birth-hut' or 'birth-tent' for their pregnant women, but in crowded communities in towns this is scarcely possible. In parts of Europe today there are still families living, cooking, and sleeping in one room, and here too, on a rough bed, the child must be born. Sometimes an attempt is made to help matters by turning the lying-in bed into a kind of canopied bed so that the woman can at least have a curtain between herself and the other members of her family at the moment of birth.

In spite of the pain and difficulty of childbirth, most women have normally had a passionate desire to augment the earth's already enormous population with a contribution of their own. As a result, fertility rites have been practised by nearly every primitive community throughout the world. One charming example occurs among the Huichol Indians of Mexico where a woman who wishes to bear a child pays a visit to a certain cave near Santa Catarina, the home of the goddess of conception. Here she deposits a home-made rag doll to represent the baby she so earnestly desires. A few days later she returns, tucks the doll under her girdle, and goes away convinced that she will be pregnant within a very short time.[39] Similar beliefs are also found in comparatively civilized communities. For instance, on a recent visit to Egypt the present authors saw barren Moslem women rolling across the stone floor of the Bektashi Monastery in the Mokkatam Hills near Cairo in the belief that they would thereby be rendered fruitful. Roman Catholics, with their special enthusiasm for material objects said to be associated with deceased saints, also accept the existence of such homoeopathic magic. One of the stranger objects they have regarded as a guarantee of fertility is the shift of the Blessed Virgin Mary, of which a surprising number of specimens seem to have survived for nearly two thousand years.

Very exceptionally fertility is not regarded as a particularly good thing, and the bringing forth of a child as a catastrophe to be avoided. We do not refer here to the incautious escapades of housemaids in the local park, but to tribes where an antipathy to childbearing is shared by every adult woman. The most astonishing example comes from Queensland, Australia, where the native women believe that the child draws a great part of their strength away from them. One authority quoted by Ploss and Bartels says that not infrequently the mother devours her child directly it is born in order to return the lost strength to her own body.[40]

The gods of birth and the cradle can only be mentioned in passing, for many hundreds are known from every part of the world. St. Augustine mentions several in his *De Civitate Dei*, where he lists the many forms by which Jupiter was known to the pagans. As an aid to women in childbirth he was known as Lucina; as Vaticanus he first opened the child's mouth to cry. As Cunina he guarded the cradle, and as Rumina he represented the breasts of the suckling mother. In his relationship with the newborn child he had many names: Educa to feed it, Numeria for teaching it to count, and Paventia for frightening it.[41] Many more deities connected with childbirth are mentioned by St. Augustine, but he seems rather to have let his enthusiasm run away with him, for the original reads as tediously as a catalogue.

Of the many customs connected with childbirth the most strange is that known as *couvade*, which is a French word meaning 'brooding' or 'hatching'. German anthropologists speak of it as *Männerkindbett*, and from this derives the English phrase 'man childbed' which is sometimes also used. Before discussing the significance of the custom more fully we will describe one of the classic literary examples of *couvade*, which comes from the charming French medieval romance known as *Aucassin and Nicolette*. The two lovers, Aucassin and Nicolette, have arrived in the distant land of Torelore, where Aucassin learns that a great war is in progress. He asks to be taken before the King and Queen of that country, but is told that the Queen is out with her troops on the field of battle, while the King is lying in childbed. Outraged by this unnatural state of affairs, he searches the palace with drawn sword until he eventually finds the King reclining upon a bed. He asks him what he is doing and is informed by the King, rather peevishly, that he is an expectant parent, and must certainly stay in bed for a month for the sake of his health. Aucassin, far from being sympathetic, belabours the King with a staff he sees in the corner of the room, and extracts a promise from him that no man shall ever again lie in childbed in the Kingdom of Torelore.[42]

Perhaps a young man in love may be excused such an impetuous action on the grounds that the King was betraying in some subtle way the conventional conception of manhood, but it hardly suggests that Aucassin was very intelligent. If he had been more curious he might at least have paused to question the King on the significance of his odd behaviour; had he been an anthropologist he would have been greatly excited to find such a magnificent example of a custom that is almost as old as man himself.

The tendency for men to become 'broody' as well as, or instead of, women at the time of childbirth has been noted among primitive societies, in classical times, and even among the civilized races of western Europe today. The practice takes many forms, but in its purest expression the husband of a woman at the end of her pregnancy takes to his bed and pretends to be lying-in. Sometimes he even dresses in his wife's clothes, and simulates the groans provoked by the pain of labour. While in this condition he is treated with all the consideration normally due to the mother, and receives specially attractive and easily digestible food. In some cases for several weeks before the birth, or even from the beginning of pregnancy, he is forbidden to handle weapons or tools or to undertake any kind of hard work. Hunting, smoking, and sexual intercourse are strictly forbidden. At last, when the child is born, it is the father who nurses it in bed and receives the congratulations of relatives and friends.

Examples of *couvade* in classical times are given by the Greek epic poet Apollonius of Rhodes, by the historian Diodorus, and by the geographer Strabo, while more recently Marco Polo records a notable instance among the people of the province of Zardandan. He writes:

'And when one of their wives has been delivered of a child, the infant is washed and swathed, and then the woman gets up and goes about her household affairs, whilst the husband takes to bed with the child by his side, and so keeps his bed for 40 days; and all the kith and kin come to visit him and keep up a great festivity. They do this because, they say, the woman has had a hard bout of it, and 'tis but fair the man should have his share of suffering.' [43]

With the growth of scientific anthropology examples of *couvade* began to be noted from all over the world. Travellers have observed the custom in China (see Plate 20), India, Borneo, Siam, Europe, and North and South America, among other places; in Africa, for some reason, it seems to be rare, although it is reported to occur in degenerate form among the Dinka of the Sudan, the Boloki of the Congo, and in parts of Nigeria.[44] In primitive tribes, of course, the matter is not specially related to our present theme of beds, for the primitive sleeping-place is only termed a bed by courtesy; but a few words must be said about survivals of *couvade* in western Europe.

In the early years of this century several examples of the custom were noted among European peasant societies and even in parts of the British Isles. For instance, in East Anglia there was a strong belief that a woman's pregnancy physically affected the man, and a young husband who complained of toothache or some other painful ailment would at once be made the subject of ribaldries concerning his wife's condition. A particularly interesting survival of the custom was also reported in a married couple in Cheshire by the anthropologist Winifred Blackman. She writes:

'The wife was expecting her second child, and on one occasion some of her friends, knowing that she was in this condition, came to inquire after her health. Having duly expressed their sympathy with her, she said: "Oh, I am all right, J — is bearing the little one this time, and he is awfully bad," and there was a great chuckling among the women. Indeed, the man suffered so badly from "morning sickness" that he was obliged to give up his work for a time, and my informant told me that she saw him going about looking an absolute wreck.'[45]

Although less spectacular than *couvade* in its extreme form, 'sympathetic pains' seem to be quite common among many married couples, including several questioned by the present authors. The transference of birth-pangs to the male partner has sometimes been thought to result from laying his garments on the bed of the woman, sometimes from a simple announcement by the nurse that labour has begun. In parts of Ireland nurses have even claimed that they can transfer the mother's pains at will either to the father or to some other man of their own choice. This they regard as a particularly satisfactory way of paying out old bachelors. Those interested in putting these intriguing possibilities to the test will find full directions in the books by Dawson, Tylor, and Black listed in the bibliography.

Many authorities have attempted to explain the origin and significance of *couvade*, but their views are conflicting. Some believe that it arose to establish a paternal right over the children in the evolution of patrilineal from matrilineal systems; others that the father took on the role of nurse as being stronger than the mother and thus more able to ward off evil spirits hostile to infants. A third possibility, now rejected by most scholars, is that *couvade* is connected with andrygony —that is, production of milk from the male breasts. Authentic cases of men who have developed full and rounded breasts equipped with mammary glands quite capable of suckling infants are not particularly rare. But it would be out of place to enlarge on such complicated problems here.

The normal product of a human birth is, of course, a human child. In the past, however, there have been several apparent exceptions to this general law of nature which have aroused a great deal of wide-eyed curiosity among the credulous. For instance, one Polish lady living in the seventeenth century is said to have become the proud mother of two small fish without scales, while Reynolds refers briefly to a case where an American girl was alleged to have been brought to bed of an octopus.[46] According to another report a child was born with a clam-like mollusc in place of a head, allegedly because the mother had had a frustrated desire for a dish of these creatures during pregnancy.[47]

But the classic example of an unusual delivery occurred in November 1726 to a woman named Mary Toft, the wife of a journeyman clothier of Godalming in Surrey. This enterprising lady, far outshining her rivals, suddenly began to give birth to a litter of rabbits. The case aroused great interest at the time, as indeed it might, and the report of the local man-midwife, a certain Mr. John Howard, so intrigued King George I and Queen Caroline that the Court Anatomist, Mr. Nathaniel St. André, was sent to Surrey to investigate.

Mary Toft had by this time been moved to Guildford, and on November 15th St. André arrived in the town full of the greatest expectations of what he might find. Before taking him to see the patient, Howard told him an astonishing tale. Mary Toft had produced her first rabbit on the 1st or 2nd of November, and between November 4th and 6th had been delivered of three more. The last, said Howard, had 'leap'd in her Belly, for the space of eighteen Hours'[48] before being born dead. The rabbits had continued to appear at intervals, and on the afternoon of St. André's visit the unfortunate lady was in labour with the fifteenth. As the birth might take place at any moment Howard suggested that they should visit her without further delay, and the two men adjourned forthwith to Mary Toft's house.

They were not a moment too soon, for the woman was already in labour, and the great man from London had the gratifying experience of delivering the fifteenth rabbit himself. He examined it closely and reported that it was the same size as an ordinary rabbit of four months' growth, but had exceptionally small lungs and a large heart. Nor was this admirable specimen the last. During the next few days Mary Toft parted with several further portions of rabbits, and also with 'a Piece of one of the Membranes of a Placenta, rolled up like Parchment'.[49] Perhaps even more interesting than the periods of labour itself were the interludes between them, when the rabbits could distinctly be heard 'leaping' in the right-hand side of the patient's belly. St. André had good cause to feel that he had not wasted his journey.

The case for the authenticity of the 'rabbet-breeder of Godalming', as she was popularly referred to, now seemed to be well established, and John Howard and Mary Toft were emboldened to ask for pensions in recognition of their achievement. Here, however, the King demurred. He directed that further confirmation must be obtained, and to this end London's most eminent gynaecologist, Sir Richard Manningham, was asked for his opinion. On Monday, November 28th, Manningham took coach for Guildford, and made a new examination. By this time Mary Toft had considerably slowed down her rate of production, and the doctor could at first find little to cause him special excitement. But, encouraged by hot towels on her abdomen, the rabbits obligingly began a new series of leaps, which Manningham later described as follows:

'The Motions were various, sometimes with very strong Throws cross the Belly, especially on the right side, at other times with sudden Jerks and Risings, and tremulous Motions and Pantings, like the strong Pulsations of the Heart; and as I sat on the Bed in Company with five or six Women, it would sometimes shake us all very strongly.'[50]

At this stage even Manningham, who had at first regarded Mary Toft's claim with a certain reserve, was beginning to be impressed;

51

but then, like many another enterprising fraud, Mary overplayed her hand. The next time her labour pains came on she was suddenly delivered, not of a rabbit, but of part of a hog's bladder. This was too much even for the rather primitive medical science of the early eighteenth century. That a woman should give birth to a rabbit was unconventional but at least conceivable in those superstitious times; that she should give birth to a hog, although even more unlikely, was still within the bounds of possibility. But that she should deliver *both* within a few hours was really going too far. The very next day Manningham moved his patient to London for closer observation.

The rest of the story is a sad anticlimax. Mary Toft was confined in 'Mrs. Lacy's Bagnio in *Leicester Fields*', where she lived, not inappropriately, on 'Beef, Rabbet, Red-Herring, and such like'.[51] Her pains and periods of labour varied in intensity and length, and although no further rabbits were voided from her body, they leaped almost continuously until Sunday, December 4th. It was then that an event occurred which finally destroyed the rabbit-breeder's reputation. The Lacy's porter, one Thomas Howard, reported that Mary Toft had asked him to procure her a rabbit, with which she obviously intended to carry on her deception with the doctors. After further questioning by Manningham she broke down and made a full confession. Depositions were taken from several villagers in Godalming (including a Quaker of high character named John Sweetapple) to say that they had all supplied Mary with rabbits at times suspiciously near to the times of the supposed births. Meanwhile the doctors had diagnosed the alleged 'leaping' as an involuntary condition of the body, part pathological and part hysterical in origin, which had been exaggerated by feigned convulsions. It had been Mary Toft's ambition to establish her reputation as a wonder by secreting portions of rabbits in the most intimate regions of her body and then pretending to deliver them as if they were normal births. She hoped she would thereby not only receive a pension, but also be able to show herself to curious visitors for money. If it had not been for the blunder with the hog's bladder she might have succeeded; as it was she returned to her former obscurity to die without further quadrupedal issue in 1763.

Although they are not as closely connected with beds as the reader of this book has a right to demand, we cannot resist the temptation to mention a few of the superstitions collected by Sir James Frazer from all over the world concerning pregnancy. One of the oddest is found among the Ainos of Saghalien where a pregnant woman is forbidden to spin or to plait ropes for two months before the birth in case the child's guts should likewise become twisted. In the Celebes the Toradjas forbid an expectant mother to stand at the door of her house, for it is believed that if a passerby sees her the birth of the child will be retarded. Any woman neglecting this elementary precaution is sentenced to hard labour.[52] As a final example, observations among many peoples have shown that there is a strong taboo on the presence of sharp instruments during a woman's lying-in. In parts of New Guinea the expectant mother is even forbidden to sew for fear she should stab the child in her womb with the needle; while in Uganda when a woman begins her labour her husband immediately carries all the spears and other weapons out of the house so that their presence may not hurt the souls of the new-born infant.[53]

A great deal has already been written by Cabanès, Witkowski, and Graham, among others, concerning the procedures adopted at important *accouchements* in western Europe and elsewhere, so this subject need only be briefly touched upon. A specially rigid ceremonial was observed at the birth of royal personages, of which Cabanès gives a full account in the Seventh Series of his *Mœurs Intimes du Passé* (1923). During the period of lying-in the mother was kept strictly segregated from all vulgar contacts, and could be visited only by her husband and closest friends and relations. When labour was nearly complete the royal *accoucheur* was expected to shout for all to hear, 'Her Majesty is about to give birth.' Similarly, while the baby was actually being born he was compelled to take time off from his purely medical duties to proclaim in a loud voice, 'Her Majesty is now giving birth.' We may doubt the wisdom of this kind of running commentary at such a critical moment, but tradition demanded that the ritual should be observed. The climax of the whole operation came when the baby was finally delivered, and the *accoucheur* had the vitally important task of showing it to Her Majesty, '*de manière à ce qu'Elle puisse en reconnaitre le sexe*'. For further elaboration of these promising themes the reader is referred to the works of the authorities mentioned above.

The next matter demanding our attention is the cradle, itself a type of bed, and the first home of the new-born child. (See Plates 21—24.) The very earliest cradles were probably hollow sections of tree-trunks, and primitive peoples all over the world continue to use very simple cradles, including crudely fashioned wicker baskets or even something as casual as a twist of cloth slung round the neck. One delightful arrangement, still found in parts of Canada and elsewhere, is shown in the illustration opposite. The cradle made from a tree-trunk was also used in western Europe in medieval times, the characteristic rocking motion being imparted by the natural curvature of the wood. Later, when rectangular models came into vogue, curved rockers were added at the base.

The children placed in these cradles were normally wrapped in swaddling clothes. (See Plates 18 and 24b.) These were bands of material wound round the body so that the baby was as rigidly bound as an Egyptian mummy. A full account of swaddling, and the strict procedure adopted for carrying it out, can be found in the Sixth Series of Cabanès' *Mœurs Intimes du Passé* (1920). The reasons for the practice are obscure, although even in medical circles there seems to have been a belief that swaddling encouraged the child to adopt the human stance, and prevented it from going on all fours. In any case it was a hazardous procedure for the infant, whose natural movements were as restricted as if he had been held in a strait jacket. One aspect of the dangers is revealed by a tale of St. Ambrose who was lying in his swaddling clothes when a swarm of bees settled on his face and began to fly in and out of his open mouth. At such a disadvantage the unfortunate child was quite incapable of taking evasive action, and it was only the exceptional perspicacity of the bees, who immediately noted the young Saint's holy qualities, that prevented him from being soundly stung.[54]

Cradles and their coverings are often mentioned in medieval accounts and inventories. Some were extremely elaborate, and were decorated by the highest craftsmen in the land. In royal circles, where money was no object, the royal cradle was almost as costly as the royal bed; thus a cradle made by command of Margaret of Flanders, aunt of Edward IV, in addition to being richly inlaid, was further adorned with twelve hundred ermine skins. Royal infants at this time were accustomed to have two cradles, one when they were on ceremonial view to distinguished visitors, the other for everyday use. But even the latter was far from being a simple, unostentatious article. One royal 'everyday' cradle in the fifteenth century is described as being ornamented with gold and silver, with a cover let of velvet, ermine, and cloth of gold. The ceremonial cradle for the same infant could hardly have been accoutred more richly, so the only way of establishing its superior status was to make it much larger; it measured no less that two-and-a-half feet across and five feet long—almost as large as an adult's single bed today.

FIG. 8. *Canadian cradles. From Witkowski (1887), p. 625*

Not all cradles were made to move on rockers, some being suspended from posts so that a swinging motion could be imparted to them. The main advantage of this type of cradle was that it did not need to be continuously rocked by hand to keep its inmate quiet; a gentle shove would cause it to swing on its own for anything up to twenty minutes. The third and last type of cradle in general use did not move at all. It was, in fact, a miniature bed or cot, used both for young children and infants. An example is the one-piece cradle mounted on castors which was used by William IV when he was one year old. This, we are told, was made of mahogany, and had 'two neat Frames the whole length of the Couch with turned Bannisters to keep the Prince from falling out'.[55]

This brief dissertation on cradles must bring the present chapter to an end. It has not, of course, been possible in the short space at our disposal to deal with every aspect of birth, but perhaps we have managed to show that it is not, as some might think, a simple question of emerging from the womb and uttering one's first cry at the misery of the world. The infants of the past have constantly had to face the possibility that they would be half-suffocated with swaddling bands, suckled at their fathers' shaggy breasts, or even eaten. Compared with adults, who can fight back, one may feel that their lot has not been a happy one, and this is in general true. But that adults also can meet with certain unexpected hazards connected with beds and bedroom life will become apparent in the next chapter.

FIG. 9. '*Angel cot*' *shown at the Great Exhibition of 1851*

CHAPTER FOUR

Some Notable Beds

HISTORY has known many notable beds, distinguished by their size, by their unconventional shape, or by the strange things alleged to have happened in them. There was, for instance, the bed used by the French physician Charles de l'Orme, which was made of bricks and had a built-in lavatory; another, belonging to Ludwig II of Bavaria, was shaped like a cathedral and is said to have cost over £ 100,000; and among other unusual designs is the circular model allegedly used by Mrs. Groucho Marx. Reynolds and other writers have already dealt at length with these matters, and we therefore leave the reader to pursue his researches in their pages. We shall here restrict ourselves to only a few representative examples to show the richness of the theme.

Large beds have always been a source of fascination, and in England we are inclined to regard the Great Bed of Ware with special awe in this respect. Its name is taken from the town of Ware in Hertfordshire, where it formerly stood in an inn known as the Saracen's Head. It was moved from there to Hampton Court, among other places, and eventually arrived at the Victoria and Albert Museum, where it can still be seen to this day. The bed is a gigantic four-poster, measuring nearly twelve feet square and rising well over seven feet to the top of the canopy. Its age is unknown, and some say that it dates from the fourteenth century. This is probably an exaggeration, however, for its style suggests that it is unlikely to have been made before the reign of Elizabeth I. That Shakespeare knew about it is proved by the passage in *Twelfth Night* where Sir Toby Belch is encouraging Sir Andrew Aguecheek to challenge Viola to a duel: 'Go, write it in a martial hand...; and as many lies as will lie in thy sheet of paper, although the sheet were big enough for the bed of Ware in England, set 'em down.'[56]

There were numerous tales connected with the bed, of course, including a belief that it was haunted by the ghost of its maker, one Jonas Fosbrooke. The ghost did not usually manifest itself visibly, but its presence was made only too evident by the pinches and scratches with which it used to harry those who slept in the bed. In spite of such deterrents people came from far and wide to try it out, and the Saracen's Head did excellent business on the strength of the bed alone. The room in which it stood was sometimes let out to ten or twelve persons at a time who wished to test the bed's capacity; more usually, however, it bore the conventional complement of two. Seventeenth-century merchants were quite as ready to think up reasons for a business week-end away from their wives as are their counterparts today, and the Saracen's Head, with its great bed, was just the place for a spectacular seduction.

Large as it is, the Great Bed of Ware is not unique in this respect, and many beds have approached it, or even exceeded it, in size. A specimen that ran it pretty close, according to Dr. Stopes, was that used for the visit to Stowe of Frederick, Prince of Wales, which was nine feet nine inches long and nine feet wide.[57] Even the huge all-in wrestler 'Iron' Mike Mazurki, who visited London in 1949, did not demand such an acreage of bed-space to foster his strength, being content with a bedstead a mere seven feet square. It is difficult to establish which was the largest bed ever made, but the record could well be held by that used for the nuptials of Philip the Good of Burgundy and Isabel, daughter of John I of Portugal, in 1429. Havard quotes the chronicler Le Fèvre de St. Remy to the effect that it was '*dix-huit piéz de long et xii de lect*'.[58]

We have hinted in the previous chapter that beds can occasionally be dangerous. We do not simply mean by this that the older and more rickety examples are liable to sudden collapse (although the male author, who weighs fifteen stone, has had experience of this on more than one occasion), but that they can actually be used as devices for murder. The most famous example of a murder-bed was alleged to exist in the inn known as the Crane at Colnbrook, Middlesex, in the sixteenth century, and is described by Thomas Deloney (who shared with Thomas Lodge the honour of being the father of the English novel) in a book entitled *Thomas of Reading, or the Sixe Worthie Yeomen of the West* (1612). This is the only source of information concerning the bed, which must reluctantly cause us to suspect that it never really existed except in Deloney's mind. Nevertheless, thirsty motorists who can resist the lure of the concrete bypass which now carries them more speedily towards the west, could do worse than take refreshment at this ancient public house which, under the new name of the Ostrich, still exists. They will find there a model of the bed, and their mild and bitter will not taste appreciably the worse for the gruesome tale the landlord has to tell of his predecessor's sinister activities.

According to Deloney, the Crane was a favourite halting-place on the long journey between London and the west country, and in those days, when horses were the only means of transport, many travellers who could not reach the capital before dark found it convenient to stay there the night. Most of these, of course, were ordinary folk, equivalent to the commercial travellers of today, but occasionally a rich merchant, a Tudor tycoon, would find himself benighted and ask the host of the Crane for hospitality. For the landlord of that time, a rogue called Jarman, this was, in the literal sense of the phrase, a golden opportunity.

The procedure was as follows. When either Jarman or his wife (for she was as guilty as he) detected that a customer who had asked to spend the night was carrying a considerable amount of money on his person, one would say to the other, 'There is now a fat pig to be had, if you want one'; to which the other would reply, 'I pray you put him in the hogstie till tomorrow.' The 'hogstie' was the room containing the famous, or infamous, bed which was situated above the kitchen, and to this the unsuspecting client would be innocently conducted. After describing the situation of the room itself, Deloney continues:

'The best bedsted therein, though it were little and low, yet was it most cunningly carved, and faire to the eye: the feet whereof were fast naild to the chamber floore... Moreover, that part of the chamber whereupon this bed and bedstéed stoode, was made in such sort that by the pulling out of two yron pinnes below in the kitchin, it was to be let downe... in manner of a trappe doore: moreover in the kitchin, directly under the place where this should fall: was a mighty great caldron, wherein they used to séethe their liquor when they went to brewing. Now, the men appointed for the slaughter, were laid into this bed, and in the dead time of the night when they were sound a sléepe by plucking out the fore said iron pinns, downe would the man fall out of his bed into the boyling caldron, and all the cloathes that were upon him: where being suddenly scalded and drowned, he was never able to cry or speak one word.'

After the dastardly deed was done the landlord and his wife would climb into the room by a ladder kept ready for the purpose and take away the victim's clothes, money, and other belongings. They would then lift up the falling floor, which was attached by hinges, and secure it as before. When the water in the cauldron had cooled they would take out the corpse and throw it into the river, 'whereby they escaped all danger'. Their last operation was to take the unfortunate traveller's horse to a nearby barn, where it was disguised by cutting its tail, docking its ears, or even by putting out one of its eyes. To anyone who asked questions about their fellow guest in the morning, the ostler was instructed to say that 'he tooke horse a good while before day, and that he himselfe did set him forward'.

Landlords of today (who would, of course, no sooner be guilty of such a deed as water the beer or offer a drink after closing time to a policeman) will find this a shocking tale. But in case one more unscrupulous than the rest should be tempted to follow Jarman's example, we must record that his sins eventually found him out. The last of a series of sixty victims was a man named Cole (after whom Colnbrook, or Colebrook as it then was, is supposedly named); he was, in fact, the 'Thomas of Reading' who gave Deloney's book its title, a man 'in a great office under his Majestie'. Now after Cole's murder the ostler went to the stable to take out his horse for camouflage in the usual way; but unfortunately the stable door had been left open, and the horse was gone. As was later revealed, the animal, 'being a lustie stout horse', had jumped several fences and had started an equine love-affair with a mare in a nearby field. In the morning the owner of the mare was naturally delighted. 'Why then,' he remarked sagely, 'I perceive my mare is good for something, for if I send her to field single, she will come home double.' And he went home with both horses, rejoicing in his luck.

But then fate took a hand. Cole's wife grew anxious and sent a servant to make inquiries in the town. The servant went first to the Crane, where they told him, according to the usual formula, that

Cole had departed on horseback early in the morning; but he persisted in his search, and eventually learnt about the appearance of the strange horse. Going to inspect it, he naturally recognized it at once as his master's, and the game was up. The local justice decided that the Jarmans could 'help him with his inquiries', to use the modern formula, and sent his agents at once to the Crane. Jarman had already fled; but after examination his wife confessed to the crime, and Jarman himself was apprehended shortly afterwards in Windsor Forest. He too then confessed, adding that as a former carpenter he had made the falling bed, but that his wife had designed it. Both were hanged, and as a final moral to the tale Deloney says that 'notwithstanding all the money which they had gotten thereby, they prospered not, but at their death were found very farre in debt'.[59]

In contrast to the murder-bed of Colnbrook, we come now to another notable bed which existed not only in fiction but in fact. This bed, which is one of the most famous in history, was the property of the same Dr. James Graham whom we had occasion to quote in an earlier chapter on the subject of double beds. Graham was born in 1745 in Edinburgh and, although he claimed the degree of M.D. and studied at the University, it is improbable that he ever qualified; in any case his behaviour had all the hall-marks of the professional charlatan. After travelling in America and France he set up in practice in London, where his genius for publicity soon had patients swarming in hundreds to his consulting-rooms. This was the age when the therapeutic possibilities of electricity were first being investigated by physicians and, although orthodox members of the profession regarded such a mysterious novelty with suspicion, the less scrupulous were not slow to exploit it for their own financial advantage. Among these was Graham, whose consulting-rooms were soon embellished with an electrical bath and a 'magnetic throne' to bring his patients the benefits of the new science. The physical advantage derived from treatment by these devices was of course non-existent, but the psychological effects were prodigious. The news spread rapidly through London's wealthier circles that the effects of this miraculous equipment were indeed electrifying in every sense of that word, and Graham's reputation soared. A man who combined charm of personality with such an enterprising use of the latest resources of science could not fail to become the most fashionable doctor in town.

Delighted by his success and the number of guineas that grateful dowagers left on his consulting-room table, Graham was encouraged to higher flights. In the autumn of 1779 he installed himself in a richly decorated house in the Royal Terrace, Adelphi, which he called 'The Temple of Health'. Two years later he moved to a new house in Pall Mall, known as 'The Temple of Health and of Hymen', which he shared rather incongruously with the painter Thomas Gainsborough. Both premises were furnished in lavish style and equipped with a vast range of electrical apparatus.

Patients visited Graham from all parts of the country, and even from abroad, to listen to his lectures and enjoy the miraculous benefits of treatment on the various machines. The Temple was kept constantly open, and by the simple formality of paying six guineas at the door the most deserving cases could enter to see the wonders within; a personal consultation with the high priest himself was of course much more expensive, but few of the more wealthy could resist it once they found themselves inside. The high-spot of the day's visit came at a few minutes before 5 p.m. when the lights dimmed, soft music began to play, and the visitors gathered together in a large room to hear a two-hour address from Graham on one or other of an astonishing variety of subjects. These ranged from 'the All-Cleansing, All-Healing, and All-Invigorating Qualities of the Simple Earth' and 'How to Live for many weeks, months, or years without Eating anything whatever', to 'a Paraphrase on Our Lord's Prayer, and a complete and infallible Guide to everlasting Blessedness in Heaven'. On leaving the house after these addresses the visitors were deeply moved to see displayed in the hall the piles of crutches left by former patients who had been successfully electrified.

We now come to the *pièce de résistance* of this elaborate spectacle — the famous Celestial Bed. This structure, for it was no less, measured twelve feet long by nine feet wide, and was supported by 'forty pillars of brilliant glass, of great strength'. It stood in a room apart, known according to some accounts as the Great Apollo Chamber, and visitors were conducted there as to the innermost mystery of the Temple. A 'super-celestial dome' was raised above the bed, on top of which were placed, 'in the most loving attitudes', two exquisite figures, representing the marriage of Cupid and Psyche. The mattress was filled, not with common feathers or wool, but with rose leaves, lavender, and oriental spices; musical instruments incorporated in the supporting pillars breathed forth celestial sounds; and the sheets, of softest silk or satin, were 'suited to the complexion of the lady who is to repose on them'.

The reader will have gathered by now that the purpose of the bed was procreation, and indeed Dr. Graham pronounced it to be an infallible cure for sterility. It was hired out at first for £ 50 a night, but the demand was so great that this was eventually raised to £ 500. The special attraction of the bed, apart from those already described, was of course its electrical and magnetic properties. Graham writes:

'The chief elastic principle of my celestial bed, is produced by artificial loadstones. About fifteen hundred pounds weight of artificial and compound magnets, are so disposed and arranged, as to be continually pouring forth in an ever-flowing circle, inconceivable and irresistably powerful tides of the magnetic effluvium, which every philosophical gentleman knows, has a very strong affinity with the electrical fire. These magnets too, being pressed give that charming springyness—that sweet undulating, tittulating, vibratory, soul-dissolving, marrow-melting motion; which on certain critical and important occasions, is at once so necessary and so pleasing.'

No wonder the bed could transform, in Graham's phrase, 'the *moment critique* into *l'heure critique*', and ensure that under 'the invigorating influences of music and magnets... strong, beautiful, brilliant, nay double-distilled children... must infallibly be begotten'.[60]

As a postscript to this remarkable tale a word must be said about the erotic performances that accompanied Dr. Graham's lectures, and which also doubtless gave futher stimulus to users of the Celestial Bed. An outstanding member of this cast was Dr. Graham's assistant, a kind of vestal virgin to the Temple, named Hebe Vestina, the Rosy Goddess of Health. (See Plate 27.) This well-proportioned lady played a leading role in the display of the Celestial Meteors and of the Sacred Vital Fire, and was even exhibited in the nude on the Celestial Bed itself to enthusiastic representatives of the nobility and gentry.

The salacious quality of the performances at the Temple was

sometimes too great even for an age which prided itself on its intellectual freedom and tolerant attitude towards sex. Thus one contemporary writer, quoted by Harvey Graham in *Eternal Eve*, denounced the whole elaborate ritual as 'an offensive absurdity and obscenity, thinly veiled by hocus-pocus, dim lights, and soft music.' He took particular exception to 'the slow dances of half-naked wenches, notably one Emma Lyon, late a servant maid in the house of Dr. Budd'.[61] Here, however, few seem to have agreed with him. The lady in question was destined to play an exceptionally important part in the later history of the bed, not least in the art of sharing it with the right people. She left Dr. Graham's establishment about the beginning of 1780 and became the mistress of Sir Harry Fetherstonhaugh, a wealthy Sussex landowner, a man with more fortune than brain. When at last even he tired of her dissolute habits and threw her out, she accepted the somewhat dubious hospitality of the Honourable Charles Greville, a well-known sportsman and man-about-town. Due partly to that inexplicable spirit of generosity towards bookmakers which seems to characterize all racing men, and partly to Emma's own extravagant tastes, Greville was soon brought to the verge of bankruptcy. However, his uncle, Sir William Hamilton, kindly agreed to pay his debts on condition that the beautiful Miss Hart, as Emma was then calling herself, was ceded to him in exchange. This was, of course, an arrangement well suited to the interests of all concerned, but it was still not the end of the road for Emma. Having succeeded in becoming the wife of a famous diplomat and antiquary she was encouraged to raise her sights still higher. Thus Emma Lyon, alias Emma Hart, alias Emma Hamilton, erotic dancer and high priestess of electro-magnetical therapy, arrived at last, a little shop-soiled perhaps but still vigorous, in the bed of Horatio, Lord Nelson, to make a small but very special contribution to the winning of the Battle of Trafalgar. With these achievements to her credit it is not surprising that her legend has lasted for a hundred and fifty years.

CHAPTER FIVE

On Lying in Bed

APART from the conventional adoption of the horizontal position for sleep, and for such disagreeable occupations as being ill and dying, lying in bed is practised for a number of other reasons. Throughout the ages these have included meditation, writing poetry, sketching, composing music, receiving friends, eating, and even dispensing justice. A few of such out-of-the-way examples of lying in bed will now be considered.

It would be possible to compile a long list of men and women who have habitually used the bed for forms of productive activity other than the purely biological aspect of creation normally associated with it. Dr. Johnson, as we have seen, used to spend his mornings in bed, and we may be sure that at least part of this period was devoted to his literary compositions. Addison, Rousseau, Voltaire, Swift, Samuel Martins, Mark Twain, and, on a somewhat less exalted level, the present authors, are among those who have enjoyed writing in bed, while Winston Churchill is said to have dictated a great deal of his history of the Second World War from the same position. *Paradise Lost* was written in bed (which is also incidentally the best place to read it, for it is an excellent cure for insomnia), and Thomas Hobbes is alleged to have worked out mathematical formulae in bed by scribbling on the sheets, or even on his own thighs.

Composers of symphonies and chamber music do not seem to have been partial to working in bed, but this is by no means true of opera composers. Paisiello, Rossini, Donizetti, Glinka, and Puccini all wrote part of their scores in bed. According to the Grays, [62] Rossini was said to be so devoted to his bed that when, on one occasion, he dropped a newly completed aria on to the floor and was unable to reach it, he preferred to write a new one in its place rather than get up. This is a pleasing story, but as Reynolds[63] gives it in precisely the same terms in connection with Donizetti, we should not set too much store by its truth.

The visual arts have also been practised in bed, particularly sketching, which is more suited to such surroundings than painting an elaborate canvas in oils. The better artists, like the better authors, have often been poor until well past middle age, or even longer, and working in bed has therefore offered them the double advantage of repose and warmth. Fantin Latour was an artist who frequently used to draw in bed because he could not afford a fire. On winter evenings he was to be found hunched under the bedclothes, his shoulders covered by a threadbare overcoat, a top hat over his eyes, and a scarf wrapped round the lower part of his face; thus fortified against the cold he would sketch for hours on end by the light of a candle balanced on his drawing-board.[64] A somewhat different type of aesthetic experience that could be enjoyed in bed was recommended by G. K. Chesterton. This was to lie on the back with several pails of paint on the floor beside one and draw bold designs on the ceiling with a broom. But even he had to admit that the procedure might have disadvantages—for intance, the paint 'might drip down again on one's face in floods of rich and mingled colour like some strange fairy rain'.[65] For this reason he was inclined to feel that such forms of artistic endeavour should be restricted to black and white.

Chesterton was a connoisseur of lying in bed, but apart from ceiling painting (which there is in any case no evidence to show that he actually practised himself), he was against justifying his indulgence by any form of activity whatever. Apart from the seriously sick, he maintained that no man should lie in bed unless he did so without a single rag of excuse; if he had some rational explanation he would be no better than a hypocrite and was likely to get up a hypochondriac.

The siesta is, of course, one of the purer forms of horizontalism which Chesterton would have approved of. Today the struggle for economic survival makes it difficult for most people to enjoy a siesta except on Sundays, when all but the most extreme Puritans feel it is legitimate, if the programme on the 'telly' is not sufficiently tempting, to retire to bed. The siesta was a common Sunday practice in Victorian times, but morality was stricter in those days than it is now and it was seldom admitted that one might actually fall asleep. To 'lie down', or to 'take a little rest' was the appropriate formula used by

Aunt Maud as she retired to her room after the roast beef and roly-poly pudding, while Uncle Ernest would plunge himself into an armchair and at least make a pretence of reading Carlyle or the latest speech by Mr. Gladstone before the inevitable zizzing noise emerged from beneath his walrus moustache.

On the Continent, of course, especially in the warmer climates of southern Italy, Spain, and Greece, the siesta is not restricted to Sundays, but is an accepted part of the day's routine. In these frivolous regions all the offices close from noon until 4 p.m., and for the latter part of this period by far the greater part of the population will be found lying in bed. Few people in London or New York would have the courage, or indeed the opportunity, of exposing their moral fibre to attack by a similar indulgence. Yet, as Dr. Stopes remarks of the Continental siesta, 'Though English men consider it unmanly, it is yet done by very manly men.'[66]

Literary men have often commented on some of the more unexpected dangers to be encountered while lying in bed. One gem, first discovered by the Grays, concerns a lady referred to by Augustus Hare in his autobiography, who

'was awoke in the night with the disagreeable sense of not being alone in the room, and soon felt a thud upon her bed. There was no doubt that someone was moving to and fro in the room, and that hands were constantly moving over her bed. She was so dreadfully frightened that at last she fainted. When she came to herself, it was broad daylight, and she found that the butler had walked in his sleep and had laid the table for fourteen upon her bed'.[67]

There is now such a shortage of butlers that this alarming experience is unlikely to be repeated, but it shows that even so apparently unadventurous an occupation as lying in bed may be fraught with macabre and sinister possibilities.

The classic example of habitual bed-lying in literature is, of course, Ivan Goncharov's Oblomov, the plump and endearing hero of the famous novel. Oblomov's attachment to his bed was so great that only by an exceptional effort of will could he persuade himself to get up at all. His laziness, combined with an habitual but quite ineffective guilty conscience, are recognizable on a less extravagant scale in many Sunday morning liers-in today. The pattern is, in fact, so familiar that it gave the language a new word—Oblomovitis.

To enjoy lying in bed to the full it is, of course, essential that one's bed should not be shared with other forms of life such as lice, fleas, bugs, and cockroaches. Even Oblomov used to admonish his servant Zahar for allowing livestock of this kind to make hideouts of every crack in the bedroom walls; to which, however, Zahar replied 'that he didn't invent bugs, nor could he see to every bug and get into its crack after it'. Even in the Middle Ages the conscientious house-wife would have tolerated no such excuses, as is shown by the following excerpt from *Le Ménagier de Paris*, a medieval treatise on domestic economy, written about 1393:

'In summer take heed that there be no fleas in your chamber, nor in your bed, which you may do in six ways, as I have heard tell. For I have heard from several persons that if the room be scattered with alder leaves the fleas will get caught therein. Item, I have heard tell that if you have at night one or two trenchers of bread covered with birdlime or turpentine and put about the room with a lighted candle set in the midst of each trencher, they will come and get stuck thereto. Another way which I have found and which is true: take a rough cloth and spread it about your room and over your bed and all the fleas who may hop on to it will be caught, so that you can carry them out with the cloth wheresoever you will. Item, sheepskins. Item, I have seen blankets placed on the straw and on the bed and when the black fleas jumped upon them they were the sooner found and killed upon the white. But the best way is to guard oneself against those which are within the coverlets and furs and the stuff of the dresser wherewith one is covered. For know that I have tried this, and when the coverlets, furs, or dresser in which there be fleas are folded and shut tightly up, in a chest straitly bound with straps or in a bag well tied up and pressed, or otherwise compressed so that the said fleas are without light and air and kept imprisoned, then they will perish and die at once.'[68]

Those who are inclined to regard the animals which sometimes share the bed with its rightful human occupant as a subject for ribald jokes are commended to read three sinister little booklets published by the British Museum (Natural History) entitled, respectively, *Lice*, *Fleas*, and *The Bed-Bug*. To begin with lice, we learn that the species infecting man are known by a variety of rather colourful names such as 'cooties', 'greybacks', and 'crabs'. There, however, their attraction ends, for they not only cause the thickening and discoloration of the skin known as 'vagabond's disease', but are carriers of such serious scourges as trench fever, relapsing fever, and typhus. Casual beds in the poorer class of hotel and hostel are a great cause of the spread of lice, and the fastidious person compelled to sleep in such places will try to ensure before retiring that no stray lice are wandering about the bedclothes.

The so-called human flea (*Pulex irritans*) is today more of a nuisance than a menace, but was formerly the main carrier of plague. In spite of its popular name it associates more naturally with animals such as the fox and the badger, which live in large burrows. According to the British Museum booklet, man 'evidently did not suffer from *Pulex irritans* until he began to occupy a more or less permanent home which must have been—and actually still is—not altogether unlike a large hole'. Many architects of our acquaintance would dissent from this last view, but the fact remains that fleas can still be one of the main hazards of lying in bed. Readers with chronic Oblomovitis may like a note of the booklet's advice concerning the odd flea that may still be encountered in bed even in the best-regulated home—or hole. This 'may with some skill be caught with the fingers, after which the fingers with the flea tightly gripped between them should be dipped under water and the irritating insect is then easily killed.'

The last animal at all likely to disturb the pleasures of lying in bed is the bed-bug, *Cimex lectularius*, which some would regard as the most unpleasant household pest existing in western Europe at the present time. The original meaning of the word bug was bogy, hobgoblin, or 'terror by night', and it is found in this sense in the works of Shakespeare and many other Renaissance writers. The British naturalist Thomas Moufet mentions it in his *Insectorum Sive Minimorum Animalium Theatrum* (1634), and one of the contributions to this early entomological compilation describes how in 1583 two ladies of noble birth at Mortlake were much distressed by the presence of the insects. John Southall, in his *Treatise of Buggs*, published in 1730, says that the creatures had increased greatly during the previous sixty years, especially in the City of London.

1. *A lady once on going to bed*
   Felt something on her knee,
   Taking a light, she raised her dress,
   And found it was a flea.

2. *She screamed, and soon disrobed herself,*
   Excepting her 'chem-mie',
   And searched and hunted, eagerly
   To find that frisky flea.

5. *She searched the bed she searched the clothes.*
   'Wherever can it be?'
   At last she pounced upon the foe,
   This little lively flea.

6. *She grasped it in her lily hand,*
   And cried 'I'll settle thee,
   I'll put your light out in this light,
   You aggravating flea.'

FIGURE 10.

Night

3. *She said her prayers, retired to rest,*
   And slumber sweet did she;
   Until she woke all over bumps
   Inflicted by that flea.

4. *She hunted high, she hunted low,*
   But nowhere could she see
   That playful midnight enemy,
   That vile tormenting flea.

7. *Within the candle fat she placed,*
   That insect with much glee,
   And as it gave a dying kick,
   Said, 'Bon Soir, Monsieur Flea'.

8. *At last she dropped off sound to sleep,*
   And all I want's 'One D',
   For this authentic history of
   'The Lady and the Flea'.

From an undated penny broadsheet in the Victoria and Albert Museum, London

This is no place to go into the natural history of the bed-bug, but it should perhaps be mentioned that, like the louse, it has been given a picturesque collection of popular names. These include the 'mahogany flat' (from its colour), the 'Norfolk Howard', and even the 'B flat'—the last, incidentally, being due to the flat shape of the bug, and not to any special musical ability it has been noticed to possess. Another graphic name is the 'red army', strictly non-political in origin, but derived from the bug's tendency to turn deep purple or dark red when gorged with human blood.[69]

But it is not only external causes that may destroy the pleasure of lying in bed. Anyone who has attempted to relax when in a state of nervous anxiety will be familiar with the condition commonly known as 'jittery legs'. Although fully extended in the horizontal position the body feels tense and unrelaxed. A conscious effort of will is needed to keep the legs still, and the keyed-up feeling which pervades the whole body may even give rise to severe physical pain. Sometimes the condition is so acute that the legs twitch and jerk quite involuntarily. In such cases the patient may feel so uncomfortable that he will send for a doctor, but an aspirin or some other mild sedative usually suffices to relax the tension.

Another disagreeable accompaniment of lying in bed may be the condition known as pruritus, which expresses itself in a severe itching sensation as soon as the warmth of the body has heated the bed-clothes. This is particularly prevalent among elderly people, but can be alleviated by the application of ointments on a medical prescription. Hay fever and other allergies may also be associated with lying in bed, due either to feathers in the pillow or mattress or (less commonly recognized as the cause) an accumulation of woolly dust under the bed. The irritants associated with dust under beds may sometimes be so powerful that the bed's occupant may seem to be afflicted by a chronic cold. These and other effects of bedding on health were recognized as long ago as the eighteen-eighties where it was the custom to stuff pillows and mattresses with pine-shavings in the belief that these would alleviate lung and bronchial conditions.

In spite of the unpleasant consequences sometimes associated with lying in bed, many people have not been deterred from going to bed quite voluntarily for very long periods. One of the present writers knows a healthy woman who retired to bed nearly ten years ago on the death of her husband, and has never stirred out of it since. There is also the case cited by Reynolds of the Frenchman, Raoul Duval, who went to bed in Abbeville in 1928 and remained there for eighteen years. The reason he gave was that he did not wish to 'see the world, nor talk nor think about it', an ambition that was, however, abruptly shattered in 1940 when the town was heavily dive-bombed. As Reynolds remarks, if Duval really did stay in bed throughout this ordeal it shows quite exceptional conscientiousness and determination. Another case of a prolonged voluntary stay in bed began in 1875 when a Spanish doctor in Galicia, being tired of visiting reclining patients, eventually decided to follow their example. He retired to bed in his own house, where he remained for sixteen years, seeing only those patients who were well enough to come to him.[70]

As both of these picturesque tales originated in newspaper reports we would be ill-advised to take them too seriously, but we shall conclude this chapter with two further aspects of lying in bed for which there is sound historical evidence: the *lit de justice* and the *lit de parade*. Throughout the centuries there have been cases of people retiring to their beds for certain special reasons, often as a result of some superstitious or ritualistic belief. The *couvade* is one example, and the *lit de justice* and *lit de parade* are others, although, of course, they are used for quite different reasons.

The *lit de justice* is the older of the two, and may be defined as the custom of a king, dictator, high priest, or other person of great authority issuing edicts and judgements to a formal assembly of his subordinates from his bed. The bed is not necessarily, nor even normally, the one he usually sleeps in, but resembles rather a ceremonial couch, elaborate in design and ornamentation, standing in some important place of assembly. (See Plate 55.) It is sometimes stated that the *lit de justice* dates from medieval times, but the institution is in fact much older. Thus in one of the fragments of the Greek historian Phylarchus, who flourished in the third century B. C., we may read how Alexander the Great used to recline and transact business on a golden bed in the middle of a gigantic tent, with his troops and attendants to the number of two thousand or more drawn up in order around him. Roman emperors and high officials also gave audience in the same position, and there can be little doubt that a form of the *lit de justice* was used by political leaders and tribal chiefs in the Neolithic Age and even before.

73

Henry Havard in the third volume of his *Dictionnaire de l'Ameuble-ment et de la Décoration* (1887—90) gives numerous examples of the *lit de justice* in later historical times. From the Middle Ages onwards, especially in France, the bed and not the throne was considered the proper place for the installation of royalty at public functions. Thus in the fourteenth century when the French king appeared in Parliament he would recline on a bed raised on a dais. The dais was approached by seven steps, carpeted in blue velvet embroidered with golden *fleurs-de-lis*. Around the dais were his subordinates, each in a position appropriate to his rank. Members of the royal house were seated, the chief nobles stood, the lesser nobles knelt; there is no record of commoners having been in attendance on such august occasions, but if they were they must presumably have grovelled on the floor.[71]

At first the prerogative of the *lit de justice* was restricted to royal personages, but the idea was obviously so attractive, allowing as it did a combination of ease and authority, that it began to be more widely adopted. In this new context, the ceremonial bed, or *lit de parade*, became an accepted part of social life in western Europe from early Renaissance times until the French Revolution. Those whose social status permitted them to receive visitors without the customary courtesy of standing up were not slow to exploit the possibilities of horizontality in their social contacts. It conferred a subtle but undeniable prestige, and paradoxically suggested a superiority of stature which would often have been far less apparent in the vertical position.

Nobles and others whose status is dependent on hereditary privilege rather than personal merit were among the first to adopt the new technique, and were swiftly followed by the smaller fry who saw in the *lit de parade* an easy and comfortable method of establishing their social superiority. Women were early in the field, and it became the practice for any woman who felt she could get away with it to receive the consolation or congratulation of her friends in bed on occasions which ranged from the death of a husband to the marriage of a favourite niece. Duchesses and courtesans could insist on the *lit de parade* as a right based on riches, social position, or physical attraction; humbler personages enjoyed it only when the production of a child conferred on them an unaccustomed prestige. Ceremonial lyings-in after childbirth were nevertheless attended by their own ritual. Guests were expected to bring the mother gifts commensurate with her achievement, and dances and other entertainments were arranged for her benefit.

The *lit de parade* also provided women with an excuse to indulge the extravagance so characteristic of their sex. It was an opportunity to wear the richest and most seductive garments and to deck the bedroom with expensive silk and satin hangings. Thus a letter written in the early seventeenth century tells how the Countess of Salisbury 'was brought to bed of a daughter and lyes in very richly, for the hanging of her chamber... is valued at fourteen thousand pounds'. Unchivalrously, the husbands who had to provide such innocent indulgences eventually began to count the cost. In fact, in some countries legislation was passed prohibiting any excessive ostentation on the *lit de parade*. In Milan, for example, women were not allowed to use counterpanes of embroidered silk, or stitched with gold or silver thread, nor to wear silk camisoles when receiving callers.

Roger de Félice, in his *French Furniture under Louis XV*, has some interesting observations on a variation of the *lit de parade* practised by ladies of rank in the eighteenth century. He writes:

> 'Long before the time of Madame Récamier the indolent belles of the day were fond of receiving *en déshabillé*, reclining on their *"turquoises"* or *"duchesses"*;* for languishing beauty with weary attitudes already existed, side by side with the more general type of sparkling and mutinous beauty: but what seems strange at a period of so much licence, these ladies, far from showing their bare feet, were expected to conceal them with a coverlet of embroidered silk as a concession to decency.'[72]

The final exploitation of the *lit de parade* by the beautiful women of the past was for purposes of lying in state. There are many records of this custom, but one example must suffice. It concerns the death of the Duchess of Burgundy, wife of the Dauphin of France in 1712, and is taken by Havard from the *Journal de Dangeau*. On February 12th the body of Madame la Dauphine lay all day on her bed at Versailles. Her face was uncovered and her hands lay above the

* Types of day-couches. — M.E.

bedclothes. That evening in the presence of her ladies in waiting (*'une obligation de leur charge'*) a post mortem was performed, but no cause was discovered for her death. Two days later Madame la Dauphine, with her hair beautifully set and tied with black and white ribbons, was displayed to the public on her *lit de parade*, before being placed in her coffin.

A somewhat restricted use of the *lit de parade* continues to this day. One well-known actress of our acquaintance habitually takes to her bed to receive the congratulations of friends and admirers after her first nights. And only a few years ago, on receiving an urgent call from a titled lady enjoying her third bankruptcy, we found her serenely installed on her *lit de parade* (the only article of furniture left) dispensing gin to the bailiffs out of potted-paste pots.

The *lit de parade* is also still occasionally used by men. Writers such as Sir Compton Mackenzie are particularly fond of it, and Christian Dior is said to have thought out many of his designs in the intervals of holding court in bed. Mr. Robert Morley has been known to receive visitors in the recumbent or semi-recumbent position. It is strange how the opinions expressed from this point of vantage always seem to gain in authority and weight.

This consideration of the *lit de justice* and the *lit de parade* must conclude our reflections on the art of lying in bed. With the exception of a few minor disadvantages, such as the possible incursions of *Cimex lectularius* or *Pulex irritans*, it would seem that horizontalism can be regarded as a generally pleasurable occupation, especially if practised as an end in itself. It may be true that once you have made your bed you must lie on it; but at least there is evidence to show that in most cases you will be able to do so with joy.

CHAPTER SIX

Sleep

S L E E P is the most obvious and universal use of the bed; we are born and die but once, and our love-making is limited by our opportunities and physical resources; but we normally retire to the bed to sleep each night. Moreover, sleep is a need we share with all other vertebrate animals. It has sometimes been said of certain vertebrates, such as elephants and fish, that they do not sleep at all. Elephants, it is true, need very little sleep, and keep in good condition on as little as two to three hours a night; but they cannot do without it, and lie down, and even snore, with the same joyous abandonment as ourselves. Fish usually sleep in a number of short naps, some, like wrasse, on their sides, others, like certain species of trigger-fish, suspended head-downwards in the water. Many animals, such as tortoises and crocodiles, spend the greater part of their lives asleep, as do certain species of mammals and reptiles which live in cold countries and hibernate for several months of the year.

The average man spends rather less than a third of his life asleep in bed, and poets as well as doctors have testified to its healing virtues. Thus Edward Young spoke of

Tired Nature's sweet restorer, balmy sleep,

and Shakespeare of

Sleep that knits up the ravelled sleave of care.

Wordsworth said of sleep:

Without Thee what is all the morning's wealth?

while the Ancient Mariner cried out gratefully in his anguish:

> Oh sleep! it is a gentle thing,
> Beloved from pole to pole!
> To Mary Queen the praise be given!
> She sent the gentle sleep from Heaven,
> That slid into my soul.

To normal people, after a prolonged period awake, sleep is an overmastering desire, and this brings certain dangers in its train. There have been cases of over-tired people going to sleep in a warm bath and drowning, or falling forward into an open fire while sleeping in a chair, while the police files are full of cases where motorists have fallen asleep at the wheel. Those who go to bed to sleep are spared such hazards, but they have to endure others, of which the most disagreeable for some people is the difficulty of getting to sleep at all. But before we deal with this let us describe some of the things that happen to our bodies when sleep overtakes them.

Although in general we appear to be still in sleep, many of our most important organs remain very active. The most obvious of these is the heart, which normally never ceases work, even for an instant, from the day we are born to the day we die. Yet even the heart does enjoy a little rest in sleep, for its pulse rate is then less than when we are awake. As a result the blood pressure normally falls during sleep, although it may rise if the sleeper is disturbed by a violent dream. The blood also tends to leave the head and accumulate in the lower limbs. This occurs to a really remarkable extent, as was shown by the Italian physiologist Bosso in an intriguing experiment. He arranged that a person should lie down to sleep on a kind of delicately poised see-saw, which was so balanced that the subject, when awake, was exactly in the horizontal position. As soon as the subject slept, however, the leg-end of the see-saw began to dip and the head-end to rise. This was due to the blood moving from the head region towards the lower limbs. The transfer was calculated to be no less than two hundred and sixty cubic centimetres.

The lungs, like the heart, work during sleep, but the number of breaths per minute is reduced. The alimentary canal, the kidneys, and the other organs responsible for filling the bladder, also rest to some extent. This is particularly fortunate, for it generally removes the necessity for passing urine during the whole of the night's repose. It is normally only older people who have their rest disturbed in this way due to the failure of the kidneys to reduce their secretions during the period of sleep.

We do not wish to labour these medical matters, but a few words must be said about insomnia, which is one of the less agreeable experiences associated with the bed. Although a cause of serious distress to many people, the dangers of insomnia can be greatly exaggerated. To lose a few nights' sleep, whether through physical or psychological causes, does no great harm, and even chronic insomnia has never yet had a directly fatal effect. The dangers of insomnia lie mainly in its effect on judgement and efficiency during working hours, and not in any intrinsically adverse effect it has on bodily health.

Insomnia may, of course, be associated with serious illness, but then it is the illness and not sleeplessness itself that causes the harm. There are also certain minor conditions, such as over-eating at bedtime, indigestion, constipation, and lack of physical exercise, that may hinder sleep, but these can usually be corrected by a number of simple and obvious expedients. Psychological factors are more difficult to deal with, but here again the problems are not insuperable. A combination of self-discipline and humour will usually assist even the most hardened sufferer to overcome his condition.

The main mental conditions causing insomnia are excessive brain activity, such as fruitlessly turning over the day's problems or planning tomorrow's work, sorrow over illness or death, fear of economic ruin, or an excessive sense of one's own sins or failures compared with one's fellows'. We hope our readers will not think us too harsh if we say that almost all these conditions are rooted in self-indulgence. Many of us have an entirely disproportionate sense of our own importance, and for some odd reason seem to think that anything that happens to our own little personalities is a matter of supreme concern to everyone else. When we reflect that life has existed on the earth for nearly two thousand million years, and even the longest-lived individual can scarcely expect to last for much more than a century, we shall begin to appreciate the futility of magnifying any personal problem to the point where it can deprive us of sleep. To accept our own insignificance, and to place even the highest achievements of mankind in a proper perspective, is a discipline which every intelligent man must try to accept. It will enormously increase his chances of going to sleep, and thus make the bed a place for pleasurable relaxation rather than a torture-chamber where, without humour or dignity, he indulges in pointless assessments of his own personal hopes and fears.

Having accepted this basic mental attitude, there are a number of practical bedroom techniques that can be practised to aid the onset of sleep. The first concerns the actual position adopted when one gets into bed. Each position has its own advocate, but medical opinion has come out fairly strongly against the back or the stomach. Left side or right side makes little difference, the important point here being that the body should be supported by the overlying knee, and that the pillow should be at such a height that the head is neither bent upwards nor lying below the axis of the spine. This position may seem so obvious as to be hardly worth mentioning, but the scientific journalist Chapman Pincher records that when he first drew attention to it in a newspaper article several readers wrote him grateful letters, saying that its adoption had given them better sleep than they had enjoyed for many years.

Pincher has various other suggestions to make about deliberate relaxation in bed as an aid to getting to sleep. He writes:

'First let the lower jaw and face slacken into an expression which would make you look vacant if anyone could see you, but can safely be done in the dark. This puts the speech muscles completely out of action—an event which is not brought about simply by ceasing to talk... Then try letting the muscles of the arms and legs relax until they feel almost numb. At the same time try to convince yourself that you are going off to sleep. A firmly rooted conviction that nothing will make you sleep will destroy the effect of any subterfuge.'[73]

A proper consideration of bedclothes is also important in helping you to enjoy healthy sleep. There are still some people who believe that an extra blanket in some mysterious way actually supplies extra heat, but this is, of course, not the case. All that a blanket can do is to act as an insulator, retaining with greater or lesser efficiency the natural warmth radiated from the body of the sleeper, or from some additional source of heat, such as a hot-water bottle, which may be used to augment it. Thus the mere act of putting, say, four blankets on a bed instead of two, may be less effective than changing two inefficient blankets for two efficient ones. The efficiency of a blanket does not depend mainly on its weight or thickness, but on its ability to retain in its pile, or the teased-up wool of its surfaces, pockets of air which have been heated by the body of the sleeper or some other means, such as warming the blanket in front of a fire. A single new blanket of good design will store far more warmth in the bed than two or three old ones with their piles flattened by much washing and ironing. It will also be far more comfortable because of its lesser weight.

We will not take the reader through the pros and cons of the different types of sheets, quilts, and eiderdowns, which are largely matters of individual preference, but a word must be said about the alleged role of the chamber-pot in securing repose. The disturbance to sleep occasioned by a long trip to the lavatory in the middle of the night prompted Dr. Stopes to an impassioned defence of this once unmentionable piece of Victoriana. She writes:

'If. . . as is so often and so foolishly the plan in modern homes, the sleeper has no chamber pot handy under or beside his bed, and has to get right our of bed, put a dressing-gown and slippers and go out of the room to a closet, along a corridor or perhaps even upstairs. . ., he will be very thoroughly awakened. I have seen no protest by any doctor, nor any public statement anywhere about the evil effects of this retrograde innovation of banishing the bedroom chamber, now so rampant among us masquerading as "modern hygiene". The evil effects on all are numerous and I am at a loss to understand how the enforced practice is so widely tolerated. It started, I believe, with a group of "superior", hard, unimaginative, sterilized intellectuals, and is encouraged by the laziness of housewives who like the saving of work involved. It is a most injurious custom and should be given up at once. I am certain it is an important cause of the current increase of sleeplessness.

Anyone who is refused a bed chamber should not continue to go without but should buy one for his own use and refuse absolutely to undertake during the night the chilly and sleep-destroying walk to the closet.'[74]

Well, this is fighting talk, and those who may cruelly have been 'refused a bed chamber' in the past will surely be encouraged to reassert their rights. Neither of the present authors has ever suffered such an enforced deprivation, and must sadly classify themselves with those other hard and unimaginative intellectuals who prefer a bleary-eyed and blundering passage to the toilet to the amenities of the chamber-pot. But anyone suffering from chronic sleeplessness might well ponder whether the absence of this article from his bedside may not be a contributory cause.

In spite of every technique to banish insomnia, a few cases are known of people who have failed to secure sleep for very long periods. Occasionally reports are published in the newspapers concerning persons who claim to have existed with only a casual doze for several years. These are usually based on insufficient evidence, or on delusions by the claimant concerning the exact duration of the periods he spends asleep. There is, however, one well-authenticated case of a patient who, as a result of overstudy, remained without sleep for six weeks without suffering any permanent ill-effects. The longest period of voluntary sleeplessness of which we can find a record was that achieved by Professor Nathaniel Kleitman of Chicago, the world's leading authority on sleep, in an experiment made on himself. By a supreme effort of will he managed to stay awake for a period of four days and nineteen hours.

Among women especially there is a belief that sleep produces a good skin and a beautiful complexion: hence the phrase 'beauty sleep'. It is, of course, true that the relaxation enjoyed during a good night's rest often causes the features to appear to their best advantage. But there is also a more strictly scientific justification for talking of 'beauty sleep'. This is connected with the substance known as glycogen, a starch which plays an important role in animal metabolism. Experiments on mice by Professor Bullough of London University have shown that worn-out cells in the skin can only be replaced when glycogen is present. This occurs during sleep, the glycogen being at other times converted into sugar and circulated in the bloodstream. Mice are not men, of course, but Professor Bullough has been quoted as saying that the results of his experiments almost certainly apply to humans as well. If this is confirmed, then the skin really will be fresher and healthier after a night's sleep, because only at that time can new skin cells be formed to replace the old.

Another interesting scientific aspect of sleep is concerned with sleep cycles, which are themselves correlated with cyclical fluctuations of the body temperature. We usually think of our temperature being 'normal' at 98.4⁰ F., but it in fact varies considerably during the twenty-four hours. The tendency is for the temperature to increase during the day and to fall during the night, the swing being as much as 2⁰ F. The periods of higher temperature are correlated with increased bodily and mental activity, those of lower temperature with a reduction of vitality which for some six to eight hours in every twenty-four normally expresses itself in sleep. But it should not be thought that these temperature cycles are precisely the same in every individual; some people 'warm up' much quicker than others, or at a somewhat earlier or later period in the twenty-four hours. This can lead to difficulties. For example, Mr. X may begin his warming process somewhere around daybreak, and it may accelerate quickly so that he reaches his peak temperature somewhere about noon; after lunch it begins to subside, and by the late afternoon his vitality may already have sunk to a somewhat low level. Mrs. X, meanwhile, has warmed up more slowly. Even by noon she has not reached her maximum, and just when her husband is reaching the stage when he wants to sit down and snooze over the 'telly', she is bright and cheerful, and waiting to be taken out on the town. The inevitable row then ensues. Mr. X points out that after a long and exhausting day he wants to relax. Mrs. X says that he should try some afternoon housework for a change, and, anyway, if he wasn't so irritatingly jovial at breakfast, when she was half asleep, he'd be more use to her in the evening. We all know the pattern, but few people realize that these difficulties are based less on selfishness or obstinacy than on quite natural variations in the temperature and sleep cycle of individuals. Professor Kleitman has summed the matter up in a phrase when he says that 'more marriages are broken up by temperature than temperament'.[75]

The reader may by now have begun to realize, and not without a certain apprehension, that sleep is not nearly so simple a topic as he once thought. Moreover, the difficulties are not restricted to the simple act of getting to sleep, of buying a capacious chamber-pot, or making sure that one's wife has the same sleep cycle as oneself. There are also the numerous hazards that have to be accepted during the process of sleep itself. This is not the place to go into such complicated matters as dreams, hallucinations, or the causes of sleep-walking, but we cannot avoid touching on one of the main disruptive factors in the nocturnal life of the bed: the practice of snoring.

According to one writer, snoring can sometimes be so disturbing that it has been the direct cause of divorce, murder, and even discharge from the armed services. It is caused by air passing between the throat lining and the rear of the soft palate, making the tissues vibrate like the reed in a wind instrument. Snoring occurs only when respiration takes place through the mouth, and is therefore particularly common among those with catarrh, or a deformity of the nose. The inflammation of the soft palate due to excessive smoking and drinking is also a contributory cause, and the activity is encouraged by lying in certain positions, particularly on the back.

The prevalence of snoring has led to the patenting of many antisnore devices. These include a leather thong which keeps the upper arm fastened to the bed-post, thus making it extremely difficult for the sleeper to turn on his back; the 'snore ball', a device attached to the back of the pyjamas which emits a loud squeak when compressed, thus waking the offender if he should get into the snoring position; and an elaborate mechanism which automatically turns the sleeper over in bed. Perhaps the most effective technique of all, however, might prove to be that quoted by Dr. Stopes from a letter to *The Times* in which a clergyman named Prichard wrote: 'No cure for snoring? We had a most reliable one at Sherborne forty-five years ago—dropping specially kept pellets of soap into the offending mouth. Further treatment was seldom needed.'[76]

Those who never like to waste a minute of their lives will be glad to learn that even their sleeping hours can be turned to a useful purpose. Numerous devices have been invented for conveying information to the brain during sleep, usually by the rhythmic repetition of words and phrases to the sleeping person. The method is alleged to be particularly suitable to the teaching of languages. Reynolds records that shoppers in Washington in 1950 were edified by the spectacle of a beautiful young lady (none other than Miss Mary Jane Haytes, the Beauty Queen of that city) going to bed in a shop window in a strapless nightgown. She lay there asleep while a loudspeaker under her pillow murmured into her ear the grammar and syntax of some foreign tongue.[77]

Periods of protracted sleep have frequently been recorded. Thus in John Stow's *A Survey of London*, we read:

'In the yeare 1546, the 27 of Aprill, being Tuesday in Easter weeke, *William Foxley*, Potmaker for the Mint in the tower of London, fell asleepe, and so continued sleeping, and could not be wakened with pricking, cramping, or otherwise burning whatsoever, till the first day of the tearme, which was full XIIII. dayes and XV. nights, or more... The cause of his thus sleeping could not be knowne, though the same were diligently searched after by the king's Phisitians, and other learned men: yea the king himselfe examining the said *William Foxley*, who was in all poynts found at his wakening to be as if hee had slept but one night. And he lived more than fortie yeares after in the sayde Tower, to wit, until the yeare of Christ, 1587, and then deceased on Wednesday in Easterweeke.'[78]

Chambers' *Book of Days* gives further examples of 'abnormal sleepiness'. Thus:

'In the middle of the last century a woman of twenty-seven years of age, residing near Toulouse, had fits of sleep, each lasting from three to thirteen days, throughout the space of half a year. About the same time a girl of nineteen years, residing at Newcastle, slept fourteen weeks without waking, notwithstanding many cruel tests to which she was subjected. Her awaking was a process which lasted three days, after which she seemed in good health, but complained of faintness. Of cases of this nature on record an over proportion refer to females.'[79]

Such cases of prolonged sleep are usually due to the condition known as catalepsy, which has sometimes led to the unfortunate victim being buried alive. For instance, there is the case of a fourteen-year-old English girl of Ramsey named Martha Southwell who was certified as dead until a tapping sound was heard in her coffin on the way to the funeral. She was released in full possession of her faculties and lived a normal life to the age of eighty-seven, habitually using the lid of her coffin as an ironing-board.[80]

Catalepsy seems sometimes to be associated with a subconscious fear of menstruation; for instance, there is the case of a Swedish girl who went to bed at the onset of her menstruation at the age of fourteen and remained asleep for thirty-two years, when her body went through the menopause, or 'change of life'. Thereafter she was able to lead a normally active existence. Another unusual sleep condition is narcolepsy, in which the victim falls involuntarily asleep for short or long periods without any possibility of remaining awake however great his effort of will. This condition is usually more inconvenient than dangerous, and the sleeper can sometimes be awakened by injections of glucose.

Catalepsy and narcolepsy are, of course, subjects for medical treatment, and are not to be confused with such manifestations of pure laziness as Oblomovitis. In really extreme cases of the latter complaint over-indulgent sleepers have actually been committed to prison. Thus under the headline 'Britain's Laziest Husband', the *Daily Express* recently reported that a lorry-driver of Hayes in Middlesex had been sentenced to three months in gaol for wilfully neglecting his wife and children by not working and not providing them with food. One of the main causes of complaint cited by the *Express* was that the offender would not get up in the mornings. His love of sleep was so great that he would often stay in bed all day, and according to his wife even had to be wakened up three times to go to court.

This may be taking things too far, but it must be admitted that one of the most disagreeable aspects of sleep is the moment when it comes to an end. To help reluctant risers to make the horrible transition from sleeping to waking life numerous ingenious gadgets have been devised. For example, in the Great Exhibtion of 1851, the catalogue contained an entry advertising the Savage Alarum Bedstead. The word 'Savage', incidentally, did not refer to the quality of the alarm, but was the name of the bed's designer, a certain Mr. Robert Watson Savage. The principles of the bed's workings do not seem to have been recorded, but it may have been similar to another equally unattractive contraption that was exhibited some years later at the Leipzig Fair. This incorporated two pre-set alarms, after which a board appeared before the occupant's eyes reading 'Time to Get Up'. If this stern injunction was ignored the bed then snatched its victim's night-cap from his head and removed the bedclothes. By this time, however, even the bed was beginning to show signs of compassion, for its last act was to light a candle and a spirit-stove to assist in the making of an early morning cup of tea.

Well, so much for sleep—how to come by it, how to survive the numerous hazards associated with it, and how eventually (if one is lucky) to be summoned by the alarum bell to face a new day. But the bed is not only a place where the closing of the eyes can translate us into the peace of oblivion or the hideous fantasies of nightmare. It is the scene of another fundamental biological activity which many have regarded as the source of the highest physical pleasure known to man. In the next chapter we shall consider the commerce of love.

CHAPTER SEVEN

The Commerce of Love

L O V E is a word with many different meanings. There is the love of God, the love between brother and sister, the love of self, the love of one's children, and even the sense in which we say we love a painting or a symphony, a town or a sport, or even porridge and ice-cream. Here we are restricted by our subject to the kind of love normally expressed between men and women in bed—in other words the art, science, or tacitly accepted form of assault known as love-making. We shall also briefly consider some of the generally recognized techniques which lead up to this potentially joyous activity, and some others devised by jealous or possessive persons to keep their partners from getting into bed with the wrong person.

Courting, which is the very earliest stage of love-making, has taken many different forms in different ages. In early palaeolithic times, if we are to accept the traditional picture, it was probably not prolonged; Og obtained Ogle by the simple formality of dragging her by the hair into his cave and throwing her on her back on a pile of skins. Such an impetuous advance savours more of lust than of love, and when in this modern age the courting period is so drastically compressed, Her Majesty's judges are inclined to call it rape and send the offender to prison. At the other extreme there are the prolonged and stiffly conventional courtships of Victorian times, beginning when Algernon first spies Hetty modestly crocheting in the drawing-room at the vicarage, and culminating, months or even years later, in that devastating scene in the shrubbery when he falls at her feet and pleads for her hand. It is natural that there should have been a reaction from such conventions, and for the last two decades the courtship period has often been simply represented by some such laconic invitation as: 'Hiya, honey! How's about rolling in?' spoken, irrespective of nationality, in an American accent. This, to some people, has the appeal of directness, but it must be admitted that the Victorian approach, frustrating as it must have been, had by comparison much to recommend it, if only because the denial of physical passion gave men time for creative activity in other directions; for example, writing long novels or undertaking pioneer work in science.

One universally recognized objective of courtship, whatever else may be achieved by the way, is physical love-making, and this is normally, although not invariably, performed in bed. What is rarer, and now almost unheard of, is for courtship also to take place in the same intimate environment; yet within living memory this was frequently the case. The practice of courting the object of one's heart's (or body's) desire in bed was known as 'bundling', a term which is defined in the *Oxford English Dictionary* as: 'To sleep in one's clothes on the same bed or couch *with* (as once was customary with persons of opposite sexes, in Wales and New England).' In fact the custom was never confined to the two areas mentioned in the dictionary definition, and has been practised in many other parts of the world. For example, its existence in the Outer Hebrides was clearly established by Halliday Sutherland during a visit to Lewis just after the First World War. He writes:

> 'Amongst the people of the black houses there is a curious custom in courtship, and, like all primitive sex customs, it is based on economic conditions. The time for making love is during the long winter nights when the young men are at home. On that bleak windswept coast it would be difficult for two people to make love out of doors. So the young man goes to the girl's house. Again, with one living room where the family are sitting, it is difficult to make love. The girl goes into the sleeping-room. There is no fire there, nor any light, because the burning of tallow candles and oil is a consideration to people who are poor. So, for warmth, the girl goes to bed. Once in bed, both her legs are inserted into one large stocking, which her mother ties above her knees. Then the young man goes into the sleeping-room, and lies beside her. It is called "the bundling".'[81]

An even more recent report, published in 1941, refers to bundling in the Orkneys, the girls' legs being tied by 'a special, traditional, and very complicated knot'.[82] It has also been recorded on the mainland of Europe and among more primitive people such as the Red Indians and Sea Dyaks.[83]

New England during the mid-nineteenth century was nevertheless the region where bundling was most enthusiastically practised. The custom inspired many poems, articles, and other compositions which sought either to condemn or excuse it, and eventually a whole book was written on the subject by an American antiquarian named Henry Reed Stiles (*Bundling: its origin, progress and decline in America*, 1869). Bundling by this time must have been a well-established practice, for as early as 1759 the Reverend Andrew Burnaby, vicar of Greenwich, gives a description of it which suggests that it was a widely accepted preliminary to marriage—a device, in fact, which allowed courting couples to decide whether they were physically suited to each other before, instead of after, the wedding.

Burnaby tells how, in Massachusetts, a suitor would ask a girl's parents if he might spend the night with her with the express purpose of establishing this vital fact. He continues:

> 'At their usual time the old couple retire to bed, leaving the young ones to settle matters as they can; who, after having sat up as long as they think proper, get into bed together also, but without pulling off their undergarments in order to prevent scandal. If the parties agree, it is all very well; the banns are published and they are married without delay. If not, they part, and possibly never see each other again.'[84]

As might be expected, the temptations of such a situation without the precaution of the 'very complicated knot' insisted on by the prudent parents of Orkney often led to complications. Thus, according to Washington Irving, bundling helped the early settlers in America to produce

> 'a long-sided, raw-boned, hardy race of whoreson whalers, woodcutters, fishermen and peddlers; and strapping corn-fed wenches, who by their united efforts tended marvellously towards populating those notable tracts of country called Nantucket, Piscataway, and Cape Cod'.[85]

The origin of bundling is obscure, but among primitive peoples it was probably a method of circumventing sexual taboos, while in more civilized communities puritan hypocrisy seems to have played an important part in its development. The less courageous moralists have always tended to believe that anything is permissible so long as sufficient concessions are made to appearances. Bundling was an ideal way of indulging, at least to some extent, the normal animal urge for intimacy with a member of the opposite sex from which even the human species is not immune, while at the same time preserving the comfortable fiction that nothing ever really happened. This hypocritical attitude was very much in keeping with the beliefs of the American Revivalist movement, which coincided with the heyday of bundling, for by some odd logic the Revivalists persuaded themselves that frustrated love-making, or at least a pretence of restraint, was more edifying to the soul than the real thing. The 'necking' parties so typical of American teenage society during the past twenty or thirty years can perhaps be regarded as a survival of this odd concept. A parallel, if not identical, attitude to morality can be discerned in the common American belief that it is more moral to be divorced and to remarry ten times than to stick to one wife and have ten successive mistresses.

The Revivalist attitude to the commerce of love was so extraordinary that it deserves to be illustrated by some examples. One of the most remarkable pillars of the movement was a young lady named Lavinia Umphreville, who reached the height of her notoriety in the early eighteen-thirties. Her chief concern was with sexual passion, which she regarded as an invention of the devil, and in a stream of fervent sermons she advocated the renunciation of normal marriage in favour of an exclusively spiritual union. 'Holy kisses' without any taint of sensuality were regarded as specially praiseworthy, and the youth of the district seem to have accepted the doctrine with enthusiasm. For miles around boys and girls began devoting themselves not only to the pursuit of holy kisses but of all that went with them, confident that every experiment was only bringing them into closer communion with the Almighty. Miss Umphreville even went so far as to preach that to forsake purely human marriage for 'spiritual marriage' was a duty everyone owed to God. This provided an ideal pretext for the dissolution of unsatisfactory relationships, and the divorce courts were filled to capacity.

So long as people were able to persuade themselves that physical desire was not the motivating force behind their activities they took to their beds at night with a comforting sense of a spiritual obligation fulfilled.

The attractive applications of Revivalism to sex were quickly recognized and Miss Umphreville's doctrines spread to many other regions. One specially enthusiastic centre of spiritual love-making was Brimfield, Massachusetts, where the leading figures in the movement were the Misses Mary Lincoln, Flavilla Howard, and Maria Brown. In this region bundling reached heights of virtuosity that have never been exceeded before or since. It was the custom for the more fervently religious young ladies to enter the bedroom of a preacher in the middle of the night, thereby placing themselves in highly compromising situations. The moral censure they thus incurred was regarded as a praiseworthy tribute to the Lord, and an augmentation of their own spiritual virtues. The clergy responded enthusiastically, and it was only when the three ladies who had initiated the movement overstepped the mark by running naked through the countryside that authority brought the practice to an abrupt end.[86]

Such fanatical aspects of love-making may strike us today as distasteful, but the preliminaries to an orthodox marriage sanctified by the Church have on occasions been almost equally lacking in decorum and glamour. We have already referred to the rather cavalier method of courtship employed by Sir William Roper in his approach to the daughters of Sir Thomas More (page 37). This practical attitude was widespread in the past, even in royal circles, where a wife was normally chosen for political rather than romantic reasons. Yet even kings and princes have preferred if possible to combine business with pleasure, and it was their custom to cause extensive inquiries to be made concerning a prospective bride.

One of the most famous inquiries was that made by Henry VII when he was contemplating taking the daughter of the Queen of Naples as his second wife. Three of his most trusted personal servants were sent to Italy with the express purpose of reporting on the Princess's appearance and character. Before their departure the King gave them a detailed questionnaire, which is too long to quote in full, but included such instructions as the following: The emissaries were to find out whether the Princess was tall or short; what was the shape of her face; whether or not she used make-up; what was the colour of her hair; whether her body, arms, fingers, and neck were fat or thin; whether she had a moustache; what was the colour of her eyes, and the shape of her eyebrows and teeth; and whether or not she had halitosis. The emissaries seem to have fulfilled their task with commendable tact and efficiency. The King was soon in possession of a full dossier of facts. Their only failure was in respect of the last item mentioned, for they wrote: 'As for such as concerns the breath of the said young princess, we were not able to approach close enough to her lips to arrive at a certain knowledge of this article.'[87] Whether the absence of this vital piece of information persuaded Henry to be cautious, or whether some of the other replies were not to his liking, we do not know. But in any case he eventually decided to abandon the project, and died five years later without having found another wife.

Another somewhat unromantic prelude to love-making is connected with the marriage of the Prince of Orange to Mary, daughter of James II, in 1677. The details are given in the diary of Dr. Edward Lake, who was archdeacon and prebendary of Exeter, and tutor to Mary and her sister, Anne. Although the whole passage is not entirely relevant to the present theme, it has such a pleasant period flavour that we quote it in full:

'*November 4th*, 1677.—This week hath produced four memorable things. The Lady Mary and the Prince of Orange were marryed on the Sunday; the Duchesse was brought to bed of the Duke of Cambridge on the Wednesday; the Archbishop of Canterbury dyed on the Friday; and on the same day Lady Ann appear'd to have the small pox.

October 21*st*, 1677.—The Duke of York din'd at Whitehall; after dinner return'd to Saint James', took Lady Mary into her closet, and told her of the marriage designed between her and the Prince of Orange; whereupon her highness wept all that afternoon and the following day....

Nov. 4*th.*—At nine o'clock at night the marriage was solemnized in her highness's bed-chamber. The King, who gave her away, was very pleasant all the while.... At eleven o 'clock they went to bed, and his majesty came and drew the curtains, and said to the prince, "Now, nephew, to your worke! Hey! St. George for England!" '[88]

At the risk of labouring the less romantic aspects of the marriage-bed, reference must next be made to two customs associated with it which have strong anthropological interest. The first of these concerns the right of a person other than the husband to cohabit with a woman for purposes of defloration or pleasure, and is usually referred to as the *droit de seigneur* or the *jus primae noctis*. The second, which we will come to in a minute, is closely related to it, and is the ceremony known as 'bedding the bride'.

The anthropological background of the *droit de seigneur* and the *jus primae noctis* is controversial, but the custom has been widely reported since the days of Herodotus and probably had its origins in early Stone Age times. In many regions the act of deflowering a virgin bride before marriage has been the prerogative of the priesthood, and has been attended by elaborate ceremonies and rites. Westermarck deals with the matter at length in his *History of Human Marriage*, and further instances are quoted by Cabanès in *The Erotikon*. One of the most picturesque of the latter concerns the custom as it was practised in Cambodia seven hundred years ago. The actual ceremony was known as the *Tchin-chan*, and was obligatory before marriage. Wealthy parents would bestow lavish gifts of wine, rice, fabrics, and silver vases to procure the services of a specially proficient priest; poorer families had to content themselves with a man of lower reputation. In cases of extreme poverty the marriage often had to be postponed until the essential minimum of gifts was collected, and to give a girl money to help towards her *Tchin-chan* was considered a good deed.

Each priest was only permitted to officiate at one *Tchin-chan* a year, and at the appointed time he was fetched in a sedan-chair with much ceremony. Often a single day was chosen for the initiation of several brides, and the streets would be jammed with chair-borne priests, each with his retinue of attendants and musicians. Streaming behind came the bride's relations dressed in their finery and carrying parasols, while the drums beat out an insistent rhythm. On arrival at the scene of the ceremony the priest would be seated under one canopy and the bride-to-be under another. Then, with the Cambodian equivalent of 'Hey! St. George for England!' the priest went to his work in the presence of any spectators who wished to attend. (The whereabouts of the bridegroom at the time are not recorded, but it seems possible that he might have preferred to make himself scarce and try to think of something else.) After the initiation came the presentation of the gifts. These were believed to 'redeem' the body of the bride, which would otherwise remain the priest's property. Finally, with a great noise of drums, the priest was carried away in his sedan-chair to another twelve months of celibacy, and the husband was for the first time allowed to enjoy the marriage-bed with the girl of his choice.[89]

But the *jus primae noctis* was not restricted to distant parts of the world. There is reason to believe that it was practised by members of the higher clergy in medieval France and, according to one authority quoted by Westermarck, Philip VI and Charles VI could not persuade the Bishops of Amiens to give up the old custom.[90] It was also practised in Russia in the eighteenth and early nineteenth centuries, and there is no reason to believe that any feudal society was entirely exempt from it. Might confers right, and where any overlord was backed by sufficient force what power was there to stop him from inflicting his will on his vassals? To our modern way of thinking it may seem strange that it was the first night that was chosen for the exercise of this prerogative (the seduction of a virgin being normally regarded as a somewhat painful and physically unrewarding experience for both parties), but here psychological factors should not be forgotten. Men sufficiently insensitive to follow the custom at all would have regarded the act of defloration as a demonstration of power rather than a source of sensual gratification. In fact the instinct for power was obviously one of the main motives for claiming the *jus primae noctis*. Only in a more sophisticated age have would-be Don Juans come to realize that seduction can be more easily and profitably accomplished at a later stage.

In really civilized societies such practices as the *jus primae noctis* would, of course, be unthinkable, and today seduction of another man's wife can invoke legal penalties as well as moral censure. Yet our ancestors in quite recent times took a far more extrovert view of the commerce of love on the first night of a marriage than would be tolerated now. In eighteenth-century England, for example, it was customary for guests after the wedding feast to visit the bride and bridegroom in bed to encourage the husband in his task and enjoy by proxy the pleasures of the nuptial couch.

The most curious of the customs prevailing at this time in England was known as 'bedding the bride', which was performed by the male and female attendants of the newly wedded couple. The bridesmaids first led the bride to her bedchamber, where they undressed her and laid her on her bed. Meanwhile the bridegroom's male friends helped him to disrobe in a separate room, after which he joined his wife and performed his duties before an admiring and doubtless ribaldly encouraging audience.[91] Few customs could be more calculated to produce impotence in the less extrovert society of today, but at the time it was so generally accepted that no one seems to have felt any embarrassment.

By comparison with such crude practices the courtship and marriage of primitive peoples sometimes shows to considerable advantage. Baron Lahontan, who was a governor of a former French colony in Newfoundland, has left us an interesting record of the 'amours and marriages of the savages' of Canada in the early eighteenth century. After paying court to the girl of his choice for several days it was the custom of the would-be lover to enter her hut with a torch and approach close to her bed. If she blew the torch out he laid down beside her; but if she pulled the coverlet over her face he had to retire. The young man never seemed to take offence at such a rebuff and simply went off in search of another girl. The girls themselves, except for 'giving their last favours', were quite willing to have any young man of the village enter their huts and sit on their beds for a cosy chat.

Apart from men of their own race it seems that the girls were sometimes also prepared to accept the attentions of the French colonists. In fact it is alleged that they showed the same enthusiasm for French lovers that characterizes some of the more conventionally minded and less well-informed women of today. Lahontan writes: 'The Savage Women like the *French* better than their own Countrymen, by reason that the former are more prodigal of their Vigour, and mind a Woman's Business more closely.'[92] Of course, this may just be Lahontan's Gallic conceit, but surely there must be *something* in that old cliché about French love-making when even savages respond to it?

The potency of men on the marriage-bed has for long been a subject of boastful and often entirely incredible claims. This again seems to be based on psychological factors, although whether a power complex or an inferiority complex plays the greater part it would be difficult to say. Cabanès quotes instances of men who had tried to pay quite unnecessary compliments to their wives ten, twelve, or even eighteen times in one night. For some, such as Attila the Hun, the attempt proved fatal, and in others serious illness resulted. Even Dr. James Graham of Celestial Bed fame, and not always the most reliable of guides, was a stern critic of this gross form of immaturity. He writes:

'It is ridiculous enough, as well as highly imprudent, for men now a days to affect Herculean feats and repetitions, when what with their father's vices and follies—and their own, few men are more than competent to the regular and moderate performance of necessary conjugal benevolencies!'[93]

Yet in spite of Graham and other more solid medical opinion there have always been men who have gone on trying to prove something to themselves by excessive indulgence. Thus a former Duke d'Orleans

'prided himself (or perhaps boasted of) having engaged in amorous combat twelve times in a single night with Mlle Deschamps. After that famous night, in honour of his exploit, he had the number 12 imprinted on the buttons of his breeches, coats, and hats; he had his shirts marked with the figure 12. He wanted to have everything in dozens: twelve guns, twelve swords, twelve settings for his table, twelve dishes on his menu. Each day his treasurer delivered to him twelve hundred francs for pocket money, and when he bestowed a little tip or a present it was twelve francs or twelve louis.'[94]

In spite of such excesses, those who regard quality rather than quantity as the proper yardstick of virility have usually felt that two or at most three 'benevolencies' on a single night are a sufficient demonstration of potency. The matter is well summed up in some old French verses which have been translated as follows:

Once is enough for a sick man to do;
Sound men can easily raise it to two.
Hotblooded gallants will go up to three;

Monks can reach five, when they're off on a spree.
Six times or seven; no gentleman's job;
That's fit for rustics, or some furloughed gob. [95]

Cabanès quoted authorities to show that hot-blooded gallantry was not necessarily restricted to younger men. Thus Charles V, 'when he slept with a fair lady (for he was fond of loving—too much so for his gout), he never went away without thrice having had his pleasure of her'.[96]

With care and moderation it is possible for the pleasures of the marriage-bed to be enjoyed to a great age. Thus Thomas Parr, who was born at Alderbury in Shropshire in 1483 and died in London in 1635, remarried at 120. His wife was a widow of fifty-two and it was said 'that she had never noticed her husband's great age, so well had he performed his conjugal duties'.[97] Of course potency is one thing and fertility quite another, but here again there is evidence to show that age does not necessarily bring deterioration. For example, in 1797 a Norwegian named Joseph Surrington died at the age of 160. He was survived by a young widow who had borne him a child nine years before his death, while his child by a former marriage was 103.[98]

One of the less attractive by-products of love-making is sexual jealousy, an emotion from which few adult men and women seem to be immune. Although doubtless deplorable, its existence has been recognized by societies both savage and civilized, and men have sometimes gone to extraordinary lengths to prevent their mates being seduced by unscrupulous rivals. Legal, moral, magical, and religious sanctions have of course been widely employed, but excessively jealous persons have not always had confidence that the chastity of their wives or mistresses could be preserved by such psychological methods alone. The most astonishing example of the lengths to which jealousy will sometimes go is provided by the 'chastity belt' or 'girdle of chastity', a piece of apparatus which the wife was forced to wear when her husband was not present to keep an eye on her.

The chastity belt has varied greatly in design in different regions at different times. The earliest models, commonly employed in Europe in the Middle Ages, were extremely heavy and cumbersome; they were usually made of iron, and were locked in position so that the unfortunate woman could not possibly remove them. Later the design became simpler, but the purpose remained the same—to render the sexual parts of the woman's body inaccessible to any man who did not possess the key to the belt. We cannot discuss the chastity belt in detail here, and it must suffice to draw the reader's attention to it as probably the oddest method ever devised for keeping two people out of bed who had no right to be there. Anyone who may wish to follow the history of the chastity belt through the last five hundred years is confidently referred to the book by E. J. Dingwall listed in the bibliography.

Although in this chapter we have so far concentrated mainly on curiosities, we would not wish the reader to think that we regard the bed of love solely as the scene of bizarre and exaggerated activities. The spiritual and sensual union between two people of the opposite sex who habitually meet in bed can be one of the noblest and most creative experiences known to man, and its joys have been reflected in many different ways in the world's great art, music, and literature.

Listen, for example, to the dithyrambic verses of Propertius in the second book of the *Elegies*:

'How happy is my lot! O night that was not dark for me! and thou beloved couch blessed by my delight! How many sweet words we interchanged while the lamp was by, and how we strove together when the light was gone! For now she struggled with me with breasts uncovered, now veiling herself in her tunic checked my advance. With a kiss she unsealed mine eyes weighed down with slumber and said: "Dost thou lie thus, thou sluggard?" How oft we shifted our arms and varied our embrace; how long my kisses lingered on thy lips!'[99]

And here again is the lusty eroticism of Ovid, so greatly preferable to the smutty limericks of our twentieth-century smoking-rooms:

In summers heate and mid-time of the day
To rest my limbes vpon a bed I lay,
One window shut, the other open stood,
Which gaue such light, as twincles in a wood,
Like twilight glimps at setting of the Sunne
Or night being past, and yet not day begunne.
Such light to shamefast maidens must be showne,

Where they may sport, and seeme to bee vnknowne.
Then came *Corinna* in a long loose gowne,
Her white neck hid with tresses hanging downe:
Resembling fayre *Semiramis* going to bed
Or *Layis* of a thousand wooers sped.
I snacht her gowne, being thin, the harme was small,
Yet striu'd she to be couered there withall.
And striuing thus as one that would be cast,
Betray'd her selfe, and yelded at the last.
Starke naked as she stood before mine eye,
Not one wen in her body could I spie.
What armes and shoulders did I touch and see,
How apt her breasts were to be prest by me.
How smooth a belly vnder her wast saw I?
How large a legge, and what a lustie thigh?
To leaue the rest, all lik'd me passing well,
I cling'd her naked body, downe she fell,
Iudge you the rest, being tyrde she bad me kisse,
Ioue send me more such after-noones as this. [100]

In later times the artistic expression of love-making is found in a hundred different forms. In Shakespeare alone we have the childlike tenderness of Romeo and Juliet, the extrovert raillery of Beatrice and Benedict in *Much Ado About Nothing*, and the blazing sensuality of Antony and Cleopatra. In music the range is equally great, extending from the innocent melodies of the ballad singer to the heavily charged eroticism of Wagner and Richard Strauss. The visual arts likewise depend on physical passion for much of their inspiration, and have the added advantage of appealing to the sense of sight—always the prime stimulus to the mating call in the human race. But whether the lover be tempted by one of Rubens' rubicund nudes or a demure damsel from a painting by Rossetti we can always be sure that if we could suddenly turn the static canvas into a moving film the two principal characters will arrive at last at the same destination: they will go to bed.

CHAPTER EIGHT

The Art of Dying

W E come now to the most solemn and portentous aspect of our theme. As the idea of civilization gradually infuses the minds of men it has become less fashionable, even in such strictly non-combatant zones as Cheltenham and Tunbridge Wells, to encourage the flower of the nation's youth to face a savage death in some muddy corner of a foreign field. The twisted corpse may indeed turn to a richer dust, but then again it may not, and by infinitely slow stages we are beginning to feel that a man must be judged by the grandeur of his life rather than the futility of his death. There is also the fact, which cannot be comfortably ignored, that Cheltenham and Tunbridge Wells are themselves likely to be in the forefront of the next battle. This has had a dramatic and salutary influence on the conventional point of view.

The transformation of the art of military murder into a science has necessarily removed most of its glamour, and as a result the bed is at last becoming recognized as a place in which a man may honourably take leave of this world. There are, of course, exceptions to this rule, and no one would wish to ask the men and women who risk their lives in scientific experiments, or in voyaging towards the stars, to call for the soft option of white sheets and the nurse's cooling hand. The risks of scientific endeavour, which constantly seeks to push forward the frontiers of human knowledge, constitute a worthy fulfilment of man's evolutionary destiny. But the fact remains that, unless we succumb to some such conventional hazard as falling down stairs or being mown down by an omnibus in the street, most of us may hope to die in bed.

Death in bed is normally preceded by illness, and the natural wish to postpone the moment of final departure for as long as possible has led to a more progressive attitude in the design of beds for sick

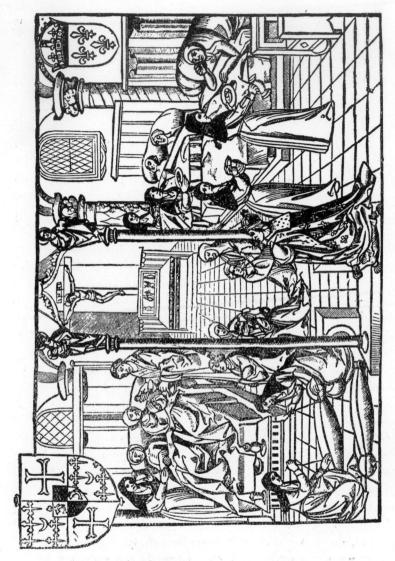

FIG. II. Interior of a sixteenth-century hospital in Paris, from a contemporary wood-engraving. From Witkowski (1887), p. 53

people. The hideous and repelling iron bedsteads of the Victorian hospital ward are giving place to more sympathetic structures, and there is a growing feeling among medical men that the sick-room should be a friendly and cheerful place rather than a sombre ante-room to the graveyard. In children's hospitals especially it is now beginning to be understood that the encouraging features of Donald Duck painted on the bed-head are likely to have greater therapeutic value than a row of black iron posts or a hook supporting a tempera-ture chart. An attractive bed for the sick is at least as essential to their psychological well-being as the bunch of grapes or pot of flowers provided by solicitous relatives. For the dying it is a minimal form of courtesy which no compassionate person could neglect to provide.

Apart from such improvements in the conventional hospital bed, a number of specially elaborate structures have been designed to allow sick people to make the best of their infirmities. One of these was invented by an American doctor named Beem, and was described in some detail in *Life* magazine for November 12th, 1945. The patient could pilot the bed like an aeroplane by means of a panel of switches. By using a different control he could raise or lower his head and feet, swing into range in front of him a washbasin equipped with hot and cold running water, open and shut the windows of his room, or summon the nurse. The bed also incorporated a collapsible table, a lamp to provide ultra-violet or infra-red rays, and a trapeze bar overhead to assist the patient in adjusting his position. One would think that such a bed offered so many temptations to the dormant Oblomov in all of us that it would be in popular demand even among the healthy. But here the price would certainly be a deterrent. The prototype cost Dr. Beem nearly £10,000 to construct, and even with mass production he doubted that it could be marketed under £600. Even so, he believed that in hospitals the bed would be an economy, for he estimated that it would cut down the nursing hours by some 25 per cent.[101]

According to Reynolds, a rather similar bed was designed for the millionaire film producer Howard Hughes when he was incapa-citated after an aeroplane accident. This bed, it was alleged, would actually move about the room at the touch of a button.[102] Reynolds also mentions another therapeutic bed with an oxygen mask for hangovers, while the Grays, voyaging into magic, quote a seventeenth-century authority concerning a bed 'to which they bring all the madmen in the country, and after some prayers and other ceremonies, they lay them down to sleep, and so they recover'.[103] This seems to be not unrelated to the technique of some modern psychiatrists, who lay the patient on a couch in a darkened room and encourage him to disentangle his repressions from the horizontal position.

And now, what of the art of dying itself? It is a strange fact, well worth pondering, that death as we know it is not a characteristic of the most primitive animals. The cell is potentially immortal, reproducing itself by the simple act of dividing in two, and life is passed on in its totality to later generations. It is only when cellular organization becomes more complex, so that sexual reproduction begins to occur, that the individual conglomerations of cells, known as parents, are left behind after the reproductive act and go through the process of death. But there are philosophical issues involved in this theme that cannot concern us in the present context. We are not concerned here with the possible immortality of the cell, but with the mortality of the higher forms of life, and particularly of our own species, which is the only one which habitually takes to the bed for the purpose of dying.

Death-bed pronouncements have been a favourite subject for anthologists, but all such collections are extremely suspect. So great is the natural determination to prolong life to the maximum possible extent that it is doubtful if anyone dying naturally in bed has ever uttered a dying phrase with the conscious conviction that it was to be his last. It therefore seems probable that most of the dramatic and spectacular utterances attributed to dying men are the pious inventions of friends rather than literal records of what was actually said. Nevertheless, some of these have such a dramatic quality that they must be considered for their aesthetic appeal alone.

Beethoven's death has been particularly well documented, and several stirring phrases have been attributed to him. Tradition has it that three days before his death he turned to two friends and, quoting Plautus, said, '*Plaudite, amici; commaedia finita est.*' ('Clap now, my friends, the play is over.') One wonders whether this is not too melodramatic a gesture to have been made by such a humorous and great-spirited man, but it is undoubtedly effective. Perhaps rather more authentic are the very last words he is alleged to have uttered, when a case of Rhine wine, the gift of his friend Breuning, was set by his bedside, 'A pity—a pity—too late.'

There is a certain unctuous and self-satisfied quality about some famous last words which rather makes us hope they were never actually spoken. Perhaps the worst example is the little speech attributed to Dr. Arnold, the headmaster of Rugby School and father of the famous poet: 'Thank God, Tom, for giving me this pain. I have suffered so little pain in my life, that I feel it is very good for me. Now God has given it to me and I do so thank Him for it.' Tastes differ, of course, and to some this may seem the highest expression of Christian resignation; but can we really believe it was meant?

Much more appealing are the simple phrases of those who went out with a conviction that normal life should go on until the last possible moment. The most famous is that of Lord Chesterfield, an eighteenth-century gentleman to the last, in his instruction to 'give Dayrolles a chair'. But others are even more attractive. Thus Adam Smith was talking to friends when he suddenly felt that his end was very fast approaching. With detached regret he is reputed to have said, 'My friends, I do believe we shall have to adjourn this meeting to another place.' Perhaps the best remark of all is that ascribed to Goethe's mother, refusing an invitation to some friends who were not aware that she was ill, 'I must beg to be excused, as I have to die.'

Women have often died well, and some of the sayings attributed to them have been very revealing of their characters. Thus we can get a very good idea of what Mrs. Garrick, the wife of the famous actor, was like when we learn that she said to a maid who brought a cup of tea to her shortly before she died: 'Put it down, you hussy. Do you think I can't help myself?' More romantic sentiments are attributed to the eighteenth-century French actress Adrienne Lecouvrer, the mistress of Maurice of Saxony, who was alleged to have been poisoned by her rival, the Duchesse de Bouillon. On her death-bed she pointed to the bust of her lover, and said to the priest, '*Violà mon univers, mon espoir, et mes dieux!*'

This great shout in praise of the everlasting beauty of passion between lover and mistress has been echoed by many dying people. Both men and women have often taken leave of the world with the names of their lovers on their lips, and this somehow seems to be more becoming than pompous pronouncements about God, redemption, and immortality. What, for instance, could express with greater poignancy the romantic influence of love on the mind of a woman than the last words of Voltaire's friend Madame de Fontaine-Martel. She asked the time, and a friend told her it was two o'clock in the morning. '*Deux heures! Deux heures!*' she repeated in a whisper. '*Ma consolation est qu'à cette heure je suis sure que quelque part on fait l'amour.*'

Many people have met death in a tranquil spirit, and perhaps serenity is the proper emotion for the death-bed. It is well expressed in the famous words of Lady Mary Wortley Montagu, who kept quietly repeating to herself, 'It has all been very interesting; it has all been very interesting.' Numerous other examples include Schiller's: 'Calmer and calmer. Many things are becoming clear to me,' and the dying words of the eighteenth-century physiologist and anatomist William Hunter, 'Had I a pen, and were able to write, I would describe how easy and pleasant a thing it is to die.'

There has, however, been another school of thought. Even philosophers have sometimes been afraid of death, and Thomas Hobbes is reputed to have cried as he departed, 'I am taking a fearful leap into the dark.' There are also the agonized words of Anne Hyde, Duchess of York, who died in 1671. Bishop Blandford being unable to soothe her, her husband approached her bed and said, 'Dame, doe ye knowe me?' Whereupon she murmured 'Aye' and then cried, 'Duke, Duke, death is terrible, death is very terrible!'

Other people, although unresigned to their fate, have surrendered at last with gaiety or wit. These utterances will probably strike many of us as the most apposite of all. For instance, there is the impatient retort of the French court physician Lieutaud to his confessor, who kept asking: 'Do you believe? Do you believe?' 'Yes,' he replied. 'Now let me die in peace. I believe in everything except medicine.' Another pleasing example is the open-hearted confession of the Marquise du Deffand who on her death-bed at the age of eighty-three declared roundly, '*Monsieur le curé, je m'accuse d'avoir contrevenu aux dix commandements de Dieu, et d'avoir commis les sept péchés mortels.*' Even an eighteenth-century Catholic priest must have found giving absolution for such a comprehensive catalogue of vices a fairly arduous task.

There are, of course, numerous other examples in this category (including Oscar Wilde's famous 'I am dying, as I have lived, beyond my means'), but to conclude this selection of death-bed sayings we return to a rather more serious plane. In our own opinion some of the most moving and insighted phrases ever to be uttered by a dying man were those attributed to the great French philologist and historian Joseph Ernest Renan. They contain a philosophy of death—and of life—which should be enough to encourage even the least bold amongst us when the time comes for us to embark on this loneliest journey: '*Il n'y a rien de plus naturel que de mourir. Acceptons la loi de l'univers.... J'ai fini ma tâche; je meurs heureux.... Les ciels et la terre demeurent....*'

This grandly simple statement must conclude our considerations of the art of dying. Yet even when death itself has come, and only the purple pageantry of the funeral separates the lately warm and breathing human being from the annihilation of an epitaph, the bed still remains. The body lies there until the undertakers have come, and in certain circumstances, even today, the bed is transformed into a kind of last *lit de parade*, where honour is done to the departed person through the ritual known as lying in state. (See also Chapter Five.)

The ceremonial display of the dead body on a bed is a custom as old as man, and the uneasy honours paid to a departed leader or sage probably date from the early part of the palaeolithic age. In ancient Egypt the belief in the physical resurrection of the dead caused the most elaborate precautions to be taken for the preservation of the body. The art of the embalmer ensured that the features of the dead pharaoh or nobleman would be kept so far as possible intact, and the mummified corpse was displayed on a bed before being consigned to the rich sarcophagus prepared for it. A similar reluctance to see the body finally entombed was shown by the Romans, who caused it to be placed on a ceremonial bed, or *lectus funebris*, for seven days after death. Rituals of the same kind have persisted right down to our own times, and within the last few decades we have seen the lying in state of famous personages ranging from Rudolf Valentino to Lenin, and Eva Peron to Bernard Shaw.

Here, then, as a place of serene repose for the shell of our humanity, the bed renders its last service. But we should remember that this solemn contribution is by no means the most important office it fulfils in the human comedy. While it is true that none of us can ultimately escape the sentence of death passed on us at our conception, it is the joyous period between these two events that the bed most aptly symbolizes. If on occasion it is the scene of pain and sorrow, it is far more often a place where all of us can enjoy the balm of tranquil repose and the supreme gifts of life, love, and laughter. It is perhaps only in this spirit that the profoundest philosophy of the bed will ever be properly understood.

Bibliographical Notes

Note: *References to books listed in the Bibliography are simply indicated by the author's surname, the date of publication, and a page reference. Other sources are given in full.*

1. Julius Ernst Lips: *The Origin of Things: a cultural history of man.* Harrap, London, 1949, p. 38.
2. Howard Carter and Arthur Cruttenden Mace: *The Tomb of Tut-Ankh-Amen discovered by the late Earl of Carnarvon and Howard Carter.* 3 vols. Cassell, London, 1923—33. Vol. I, pp. 110—11.
3. Gray, C. and M. (1946), pp. 19—20.
4. Fosbroke (1825), Vol. I, p. 226.
5. Fosbroke (1825), Vol. I, p. 227.
6. Havard (1887—90), Vol. 3, cols. 454—5.
7. *The Book of Ser Marco Polo, the Venetian, concerning the Kingdoms and Marvels of the East.* Newly translated and edited, with notes, by Colonel Henry Yule. 2 vols. London, 1871. Vol. 2, p. 282.
8. Stopes (1956), p. 23.
9. Leonardo da Vinci: *The Notebooks of Leonardo da Vinci.* Rendered into English and introduced by Edward MacCurdy. 2 vols. Cape, London, 1938. Vol. 2, p. 516.
10. Stopes (1956), pp. 30—1.
11. Fosbroke (1825), Vol. I, pp. 227—8.
12. Reynolds (1952), p. 107.
13. Stopes (1956), p. 39.
14. Kenneth Little: 'Values in Primitive Society.' *The Listener.* London, September 14th, 1950, Vol. 44, No. 1128, p. 336.
15. Reynolds (1952), pp. 155—6.
16. Wilhelm Heinrich Immanuel Bleek: *A Brief Account of Bushman Folklore, and other texts.* London, 1875. p. 19.
17. Frazer (1911—36), Vol. I, p. 123.

18. Alcide Dessalines d'Orbigny: *Voyage dans l'Amérique meridionale—la Brésil, la République orientale de l'Uruguay, la République Argentine, la Patagonie, la République du Chili, la République de Bolivia, la République du Pérou—executé pendant les années 1826, 1827, 1828, 1829, 1830, 1831, 1832 et 1833, par A. d'Orbigny.* 9 vols. Paris; Strasbourg, 1835—47. Vol. 3, Part I, p. 226.

19. Richard Carrington: *Elephants: a short account of their natural history, evolution, and influence on mankind.* Chatto and Windus, London, 1958. p. 239.

20. Frazer (1911—36), Vol. 1, p. 213.

21. Stopes (1956), pp. 33—4.

22. Reynolds (1952), pp. 84—5.

23. Stopes (1956), pp. 45—6.

24. Graham, J. (1783), p. 11.

25. Reynolds (1952), p. 91.

26. Cunnington, C. W. and P. (1951), p. 23.

27. John Aubrey: *Aubrey's Brief Lives.* Edited from the original manuscripts and with an introduction by Oliver Lawson Dick. Secker and Warburg, London, 1949. p. 214.

28. Cunnington, C. W. and P. (1951), p. 43.

29. Stopes (1956), pp. 48—9.

30. Edward Gibbon: *The History of the Decline and Fall of the Roman Empire.* Edited with introduction, notes and appendices by J. B. Bury. Second edition; 7 vols. Methuen, London, 1926—9. Vol. 2, Ch. 15, pp. 38—40.

31. Gray, C. and M. (1946), p. 81.

32. Elizabeth Cleghorn Gaskell: *Cranford.* The World's Classics. Humphrey Milford, Oxford University Press, London, 1934. p. 148.

33. *Boswell's Life of Johnson.* 2 vols. Humphrey Milford, Oxford University Press, London, 1933. Vol. 2, p. 178.

34. Walter de la Mare: *Behold this Dreamer: of reverie, night, sleep, dream, love-dreams, nightmare, death, the unconscious, the imagination, divination, the artist, and kindred subjects.* Faber, London, 1939. p. 35, note 1.

35. Research conducted by the Vermont and Indiana Experiment Stations of the U.S. Department of Agriculture. See report in *The Philadelphia Inquirer,* quoted in *Science Digest,* Chicago, April 1949. p. 72.

36. *Time*, New York and London, January 14th, 1946. Vol. 47, No. 2, p. 10.
37. Gray, C. and M. (1946), p. 147.
38. Ploss, Bartels and Bartels (1935), Vol. 2, p. 564.
39. Frazer (1911—36), Vol. I, p. 71.
40. Ploss, Bartels and Bartels (1935), Vol. 2, p. 533.
41. Saint Augustine: *The City of God*. Translated by John Healey, with an introduction by Ernest Barker. Dent, London, 1931. Book 4, Ch. 11, p. 181.
42. *Aucassin and Nicolette and other Mediaeval Romances and Legends*. Translated from the French with an introduction by Eugene Mason. Everyman's Library. Dent, London, 1910. pp. 29—30.
43. *The Book of Ser Marco Polo, the Venetian, concerning the Kingdoms and Marvels of the East*. Newly translated and edited, with notes, by Colonel Henry Yule. 2 vols. London, 1871. Vol. 2, p. 52.
44. Dawson (1929), pp. 16—18.
45. Winifred Susan Blackman: 'Traces of Couvade (?) in England.' *Folk-lore*, Vol. 29, 1918, p. 320. Published for the Folk-Lore Society by Sidgwick and Jackson, London.
46. Reynolds (1952), p. 15, note 1.
47. Graham, H. (1950), p. 334.
48. Saint Andrè (1727), p. 5.
49. Saint Andrè (1727), pp. 29—30.
50. Manningham (1726), pp. 10—11.
51. Manningham (1726), p. 22.
52. Frazer (1911—36), Vol. 1, p. 114.
53. Frazer (1911—36), Vol. 3, pp. 238—9.
54. Macquoid and Edwards (1954), Vol. 2, p. 148.
55. Macquoid and Edwards (1954), Vol. 2, p. 154.
56. Shakespeare: *Twelfth Night*, Act 3, Sc. 2, lines 39—45.
57. Stopes (1956), pp. 29—30.
58. Havard (1887—90), Vol. 3, col. 412.
59. Thomas Deloney: *Thomas of Reading, or the sixe worthy yeomen of the West*. Now the fourth time corrected and enlarged, by T.D. London, 1612. Ch. 11 (the pages are not numbered).
60. Graham, J. (1783), p. 20.
61. Graham, H. (1950), p. 373.

62. Gray, C. and M. (1946), p. 12.

63. Reynolds (1952), p. 6.

64. William Gaunt: *The Aesthetic Adventure*. Cape, London, 1945. p. 29.

65. Chesterton (1930), p. 49.

66. Stopes (1956), p. 13.

67. August John Carpenter Hare: *The Story of My Life*. 6 vols. London, 1896—1900. Vol. 5, p. 295.

68. *Le Ménagier de Paris, traité de morale et d'économie domestique composé vers 1393 par un bourgeois Parisien*. Edited with an introduction by Baron Jérome Frédéric Pichon. 2 vols. Paris, 1846. The present translation is by Eileen Power in *Medieval People*. Seventh edition, revised. Methuen, London, 1939. p. 102.

69. Publications 2a (1954), 3a (1958), and 5 (1954) in the Economic Series of the British Museum (Natural History).

70. Reynolds (1952), pp. 63—4.

71. Havard (1887—90), Vol. 3, cols. 399—411.

72. Félice (1920a), p. 104.

73. Pincher (1954), p. 57.

74. Stopes (1956), pp. 118—19.

75. Kleitman (1939), Part 3, pp. 191—279, contains a full discussion of these matters.

76. Stopes (1956), p. 120.

77. Reynolds (1952), p. 65.

78. John Stow: *A Survey of London*. Reprinted from the text of 1603 with introduction and notes by Charles Lethbridge Kingsford; 2 vols. Clarendon Press, Oxford, 1908. Vol. 1, p. 59.

79. *The Book of Days: a miscellany of popular antiquities, etc.* Edited by R. Chambers. 2 vols. W. and R. Chambers, London and Edinburgh, 1888. Vol. 1, p. 557.

80. Pincher (1954), p. 94.

81. Halliday Sutherland: *The Arches of the Years*. Bles, London, 1933. pp. 290—1.

82. *Daily Mail*, London, January 6th, 1941, quoted in Reynolds (1952), p. 188.

83. Turner (1954), p. 122.

84. Quoted in Turner (1954), p. 124.

85. Quoted in Reynolds (1952), p. 189.

86. See Ray Strachey's introduction to *Religious Fanaticism: extracts from the papers of Hannah Whitall Smith*. Faber and Gwyer, London, 1928. pp. 54—5.

87. Cabanès (1903—9), Series 5, pp. 71—6.

88. *Diary of Dr. Edward Lake, Archdeacon and Prebendary of Exeter, Chaplain and Tutor of the Princesses Mary and Anne, daughters of the Duke of York, afterwards James the Second: in the years 1677—1678.* Edited by George Percy Elliott. Printed for the Camden Society, 1846. *Camden Miscellany*, London, Vol. 1, 1847, pp. 5—6.

89. Cabanès (1933), pp. 24—6.

90. Westermarck (1891), p. 77, note 5.

91. Scott (1953), pp. 227—8.

92. Louis Armand de Lom d'Arce, Baron de Lahontan: *New Voyages to North-America, giving a full account of the customs, commerce, religion, and strange opinions of that country, etc.* Second edition; 2 vols. London, 1735. Vol. 2, pp. 36—47.

93. Graham, J. (*c.* 1783), p. 3, note.

94. Cabanès (1933), p. 247, quoting Turin.

95. Cabanès (1933), p. 247, note.

96. Cabanès (1933), p. 247, quoting Brantôme.

97. Cabanès (1933), p. 244, quoting Hufeland.

98. Cabanès (1933), p. 245.

99. *The Elegies of Propertius.* With an English translation by H. E. Butler. Loeb Classical Library. Heinemann, London, 1952. pp. 103—5.

100. Ovid: *Elegy 5.* Translated by Christopher Marlowe.

101. *Life*, New York and London, November 12th, 1945. Vol. 19, Part 3, pp. 92—3.

102. Reynolds (1952), pp. 107—8.

103. Gray, C. and M. (1946), p. 121.

Bibliography

B.U. ENCYCLOPAEDIC HANDBOOK TO THE BEDDING AND UPHOLSTERY INDUSTRY. Bedding Publications, London. (Current issue.)

BARTELS, MAX. See PLOSS, HERMANN HEINRICH.

BARTELS, PAUL. See PLOSS, HERMANN HEINRICH.

BEGA, *pseud.* (1930): *Last Words of Famous Men.* Williams and Norgate, London.

BELL, J. MUNRO (1938): *The Furniture Designs of Chippendale, Hepplewhite and Sheraton.* Arranged by J. Munro Bell with an introduction and critical estimate by Arthur Hayden and an essay by Charles Messer Stow. The Cresset Press, London.

BIRRELL, FRANCIS FREDERICK LOCKER, and LUCAS, FRANK LAURENCE (1930): *The Art of Dying: an anthology.* The Hogarth Press, London.

BLACK, WILLIAM GEORGE (1883): *Folk Medicine: a chapter in the history of culture.* London.

BRITISH MUSEUM ((NATURAL HISTORY) (1954a): *The Bed-Bug: its habits and life history and how to deal with it.* Economic Series, No. 5. Seventh edition. Trustees of the British Museum, London.

BRITISH MUSEUM (NATURAL HISTORY) (1954b): *Lice.* Economic Series, No. 2a. Third edition. Trustees of the British Museum, London.

BRITISH MUSEUM (NATURAL HISTORY) (1958): *Fleas: their medical and veterinary importance.* Economic Series, No. 3a. Trustees of the British Museum, London.

BRODHURST, JAMES GEORGE JOSEPH PENDEREL. See PENDEREL-BRODHURST.

C.R. (1698): *The Compleat Midwife's Practice enlarged, in the most weighty and high concernments of the Birth of Man. Containing a perfect Directory or Rules for Midwives and Nurses, etc.* Fifth edition, corrected and enlarged by John Pechey. London.

CABANÈS, AUGUSTIN (1897): *The Secret Cabinet of History peeped into by a doctor.* Translated by W. C. Costello and preceded by a letter of M. Victorien Sardou. Paris. pp. 81—104: 'The First Pregnancy of Marie Antoinette'; pp. 179—90: 'The Accouchement of the Empress Marie-Louise'.

115

CABANÈS, AUGUSTIN (1898): *Curious Bypaths of History, being medico-historical studies and observations by Dr. Cabanès.* Paris. pp. 57—74: 'The First Accoucheur at the Court of Louis XIV'.

CABANÈS, AUGUSTIN (1903—9): *Les Indiscrétions de l'Histoire.* Paris. 6 series. Series 1, 1903, Pt. 1, Ch. 1, pp. 3—32: 'De Quand date la Chemise de Nuit?' Series 5, 1908, Pt. 2, Ch. 1, pp. 71—6: 'Une Enquête Matrimoniale au Sezieme Siècle'.

CABANÈS, AUGUSTIN (1920): *Moeurs Intimes du Passé.* Series 6. Paris.

CABANÈS, AUGUSTIN (1923): *Moeurs Intimes du Passé.* Series 7. Paris.

CABANÈS, AUGUSTIN (1933): *The Erotikon. Being an illustrated treasury of scientific marvels of human sexuality.* Translated from the French by Robert Meadows. Falstaff Press, New York.

CHESTERTON, GILBERT KEITH (1930): 'On Lying in Bed', in *Tremendous Trifles.* Twelfth edition. Methuen, London.

CHIPPENDALE, THOMAS. See BELL, J. MUNRO.

COMPLEAT MIDWIFE'S PRACTICE, THE. See C.R.

CRÉBILLON, CLAUDE PROSPER JOLYOT DEO See JOLYOT DE CRÉBILLON.

CUNNINGTON, CECIL WILLETT, and CUNNINGTON, PHILLIS (1951): *The History of Underclothes.* Michael Joseph, London.

DAWSON, WARREN ROYAL (1929): *The Custom of Couvade.* Publications of the University of Manchester, No. 194, Ethnological series, No. 4. Manchester University Press, Manchester.

DINGWALL, ERIC JOHN (1931): *The Girdle of Chastity: a medico-historical study.* Routledge, London.

EDWARDS, HERBERT CECIL RALPH. See MACQUOID, PERCY.

FÉLICE, ROGER DE (1920a): *French Furniture under Louis XV.* Translated by Florence Simmonds. Heinemann, London.

FÉLICE, ROGER DE (1920b): *French Furniture Under Louis XVI.* Translated by F. M. Atkinson. Heinemann, London.

FÉLICE, ROGER DE (1923): *French Furniture in the Middle Ages and Under Louis XIII.* Translated by F. M. Atkinson. Heinemann, London.

FÉLICE, ROGER DE (1927): *French Furniture Under Louis XIV.* Translated by F. M. Atkinson. Heinemann, London.

FOSBROKE, THOMAS DUDLEY (1825): *Encyclopaedia of Antiquities and Elements of Archaelogy, classical and mediaeval.* 2. vols. London. Vol. 1, pp. 226—7: 'Beds, Bedsteads'; Vol. 1, pp. 227—9: 'Beds, Bedding'.

FRAZER, JAMES GEORGE (1910): *Totemism and Exogamy.* London. Vol. 1, p. 73; Vol. 4, pp. 244—55: 'Couvade'.

FRAZER, JAMES GEORGE (1911—36): *The Golden Bough: a study in magic and religion.* Third edition; 13 vols. Macmillan, London.

FURNISHER'S ENCYCLOPAEDIA, THE (1953). Edited by Michael Sheridan. National Trade Press, London. Third section, pp. 119—48: 'Beds and Bedding'.

GILLESPIE, ROBERT DICK (1929): *Sleep, and the treatment of its disorders.* Baillière, London.

GRAHAM, HARVEY, *pseud.* [i.e. DR. ISAAC HARVEY FLACK] (1950): *Eternal Eve.* [On the history of obstetrics.] Heinemann Medical Books, London.

GRAHAM, HARVEY, *pseud.* [i.e. DR. ISAAC HARVEY FLACK] (1952): *A Doctor's London.* Allan Wingate, London.

GRAHAM, JAMES (1783): *A Lecture on the Generation, Increase and Improvement of the Human Species! interspersed with precepts for the preservation and exaltation of personal beauty and loveliness, etc.* London.

GRAHAM, JAMES (*c.* 1783): *Private Medical Advice to Married Ladies and Gentlemen.* London.

GRAY, CECIL, and GRAY, MARGERY (1946): *The Bed, or the clinophile's vade mecum.* Decorated by Michael Ayrton. Nicholson and Watson, London.

HAVARD HENRY (1887— 90): *Dictionnaire de l'Ameublement et de la Décoration depuis le XIIIᵉ siècle jusqu'à nos jours.* 4 vols. Paris. Vol. 3, cols. 370—455: 'Lit.'

HEPPLEWHITE, GEORGE. See BELL, J. MUNRO.

JOLYOT DE CRÉBILLON, CLAUDE PROSPER (1781): *The Sopha: a moral tale.* Translated from the French; 2 vols. London.

KANG, YOUNGHILL (1958): 'Bed'. Article in *Encyclopaedia Britannica,* Vol. III, pp. 292—4 (first part adapted from Penderel-Brodhurst's article in the thirteenth edition, *q.v.*). London.

KLEITMAN, NATHANIEL (1939): *Sleep and Wakefulness as alternating phases in the cycle of existence.* University of Chicago Monographs in Medicine, University of Chicago Press, Chicago.

LOCKWOOD, SARAH M. (1925): *Antiques.* [With special reference to early American furniture.] Heinemann, London. pp. 5—8: 'Beds'.

LUCAS, FRANK LAURENCE. See BIRRELL, FRANCIS FREDERICK LOCKER.

MACNISH, ROBERT (1830): *The Philosophy of Sleep.* Glasgow.

MACQUOID, PERCY, and EDWARDS, HERBERT CECIL RALPH (1954): *The Dictionary of English Furniture.* Second edition, revised; 3 vols. *Country Life,* London. Vol. 1, pp. 36—67: 'Beds'; Vol. 1, pp. 67—9: 'Angel Beds, Field Beds,

117

Livery Beds, etc.'; Vol. 2, pp. 134—46: 'Couches and Day Beds'; Vol. 2, pp. 148—54: 'Cradles'.

MANNINGHAM, RICHARD (1726): *An exact Diary of what was observ'd during a close attendance upon Mary Toft, the pretended Rabbet-Breeder of Godalming in Surrey from Monday Nov. 28, to Wednesday Dec. 7 following. Together with an account of her confession of the fraud.* London. [Bound with many other pamphlets on the same subject in *Tracts Relating to Mary Toft* in the Reading Room of the British Museum, London.]

MARX, GROUCHO (1930): *Beds.* Farrar and Rinehart, New York.

PENDEREL–BRODHURST, JAMES GEORGE JOSEPH (1926): 'Bed'. Article in *Encyclopaedia Britannica,* thirteenth edition, Vol. III, pp. 612—13. Cambridge. See also KANG, YOUNGHILL (1958).

PINCHER, HENRY CHAPMAN (1954): *Sleep: how to get more of it.* Illustrations by Artie. Daily Express, London.

PLOSS, HERMANN HEINRICH; BARTELS, MAX, and BARTELS, PAUL (1935): *Woman: an historical gynaecological and anthropological compendium.* Edited and translated by Eric John Dingwall. 3 vols. Heinemann Medical Books, London. Vol. 2, Part C: 'Woman in the Sex Relationship'.

REYNOLDS, REGINALD (1952): *Beds: with many noteworthy instances of lying on, under or about them.* Deutsch, London.

ROE, FREDERICK GORDON (1949): *English Cottage Furniture.* Phoenix House, London.

ROGERS, JOHN CHARLES (1950): *English Furniture.* Revised and enlarged by Margaret Jourdain. Country Life, London.

SAINT ANDRÉ, NATHANIEL (1727): *A short narrative of an extraordinary delivery of Rabbets, perform'd by Mr. John Howard, Surgeon at Guilford.* London. [Bound with many other pamphlets on the same subject in *Tracts Relating to Mary Toft* in the Reading Room of the British Museum, London.]

SCOTT, GEORGE RYLEY (1953): *Curious Customs of Sex and Marriage: an inquiry relating to all races and nations from antiquity to the present day.* Torchstream Books, London.

SHERATON, THOMAS. See BELL, J. MUNRO.

SHERIDAN, MICHAEL. See THE FURNISHER'S ENCYCLOPAEDIA.

SOUTHALL, JOHN (1730): *A Treatise of Buggs, shewing when and how they were first brought into England.* London.

STILES, HENRY REED (1869): *Bundling: its origin, progress and decline in America.* Albany, New York.

STOPES, MARIE CARMICHAEL (1956): *Sleep*. Chatto and Windus, London.

TOFT, MARY. *Tracts relating to Mary Toft*. See SAINT ANDRÉ, NATHANIEL, and MANNINGHAM, RICHARD.

TURNER, ERNEST SACKVILLE (1954): *A History of Courting*. Michael Joseph, London.

TYLOR, EDWARD BURNETT. (1865): *Researches into the Early History of Mankind, and the development of civilization*. London. pp. 287—97: 'Couvade'.

VESTINA, HEBE, *pseud*. (1782): *Il Convito Amoroso! or a Serio-comico-philosophical Lecture on the Causes, Nature, and Effects of Love and Beauty... as Delivered by Hebe Vestina, the rosy Goddess of Youth and Health! From the Electrical Thrones in the Great Apollo Chamber, at the Temple of Hymen in London,... to which is subjoined, a Description of the stupendous Nature and Effects of the Celebrated Celestial Bed!* Second edition. London.

VIOLLET-LE-DUC, EUGÈNE EMMANUEL (1855—8): *Dictionnaire raisonné du Mobilier Français de l'époque carlovingienne à la Rénaissance*. 6 vols. Paris. Vol. 1: 'Meubles', pp. 171—87: 'Lit'.

WESTERMARCK, EDWARD (1891): *The History of Human Marriage*. London.

WITKOWSKI, GUSTAVE JOSEPH ALPHONSE (1887): *Histoire des Accouchements chez tous les peuples*. Paris.

Index

Index

*Page numbers printed in italics refer to figures in the text.
References to the artists responsible for the principal plates
and drawings are included.*

Aborigines, Australian, 33
Accouchements, royal, 53
Addison, Joseph, 65
Ainos, 53
Alarms, 86
Albert, Prince Consort, Plate 72*a*
Aldhelm, St., of Malmesbury, 40
Alexander the Great, 73
Ambrose, St., 54
Apollonius of Rhodes, 48
Architectile, 21
Arnold, Dr., 105
Artists who worked in bed, 66
Assyrian beds, 18
Attila the Hun, 97
Aubrey, John, 37
Augustine, St., 47
Authors who worked in bed, 65

Bardo Palace, Plate 28
Beauty sleep, 82
Bed, on wheels, *21*; of Ware, 22,
57—8, Plate 26*c*; mechanical, 26;
of nails, 28, Plate 16*b*; warming,
34; sharing, 35, 39—40; camp,
36; entering, 41; leaving, 42;
eating in, 43; making, 43; circular,
57; as device for murder, 58—61,
Plates 26*a* and 26*b*; Celestial,
62—3; lying in, 65—76, Plates

49—53; working in, 65—6; lengthy
stays in, 72; folding, from Egypt,
Plates 3*a* and 3*b*; travelling in,
Plate 13*b*; of Bey of Tunis, Plate
28; of Empress Josephine, Plate
29; summer, Plate 30; eliptic,
Plate 31
Bed-bugs, 68, 71
Bedding, 28—30; superstitions con-
cerning, 32—3; effect on health,
72; effect on sleep, 80—1
Bedding the bride, 94, 95—6
Bed-lamps, medieval, 20
Bed-lice, 68, 71
Bed-mats, 17
Beds, primitive, 17—18; Egyptian,
18, Plate 3; Assyrian, 18; Median,
18; Persian, 18; Greek, 19, 35;
Roman, 19, 35; Saxon, 20, *21*;
German, 19, 20, Plate 6; medieval,
19, 20—1, *21*, *36*, Plates 4, 13*a*, 17,
18, 49, 58, 67*a* and 71*a*; French,
22—4, *23*, Plates 8, 12*a*, 12*b*, 17,
29, 68, 69 and 71*a*; English, 24*ff*,
Plates 7, 9, 10, 11, 15*b*, 25, 26*c*, 30,
31, 32 and 50; Italian, 24, Plate
5*a*; Indian, 27—8, Plate 67*b*;
Chinese, 27; Japanese, 27—8;
superstitions concerning, 32—3;
odd uses for, 43, notable

57—64, Plates 25—32; hospital, *102*, 103

Beem, Dr., 103

Beethoven, Ludwig von, 104

Behan, Brendan, Plate 61

Bernelle, Agnes, Plate 51

Birth, 44*ff*; of Brahma, *44*; in classical times, 45; gods of, 46—7; of quadruplets, Plate 18; of a fine boy, Plate 19*a*; of rabbits, Plate 19*b*

Birth-hut, 46

Blackman, Winifred, 49

Blankets, 29—30; electric, 34; as aids to sleep, 80—1

Bleek, Wilhelm, 32

Boilly, L. L., Plate 68

Boloki, 49

Bolsters, 30

Bonnard, Pierre, Plate 48

Bonnivet, Admiral, 41

Borde, Andrew, 38

Bosse, Abraham, Plate 19*a*

Bosso, 78

Boucher, François, Plate 37*a*

Brahma, birth of, *44*

Brown, Maria, 92

Buffon, Comte de, 42

Bugs, 68, 71—2

Bullough, W. S., 82

Bundling, 89—91

Burnaby, Andrew, 9

Bushmen, 32

Cabanès, Augustin, 53, 94, 97, 98

Caesarian operation, *45*

Camm, F. J., model by, Plates 26*a* and 26*b*

Camp bed, *36*

Carnarvon, Lord, 18

Carpaccio, Vittore, Plate 5*a*

Carter, Howard, 18

Caruso, Enrico, 30

Catalepsy, 85

Celestial Bed, 62—3

Chamber-pots, 81

Chaponnier, Plate 68

Chares of Mytilene, 19

Charles V, 98

Charles VIII of France, 41

Charpoy, 28

Chastity belts, 98—9

Chesterfield, Lord, 105

Chesterton, G. K., 66

China, *couvade* in, Plate 20

Chinese beds, 27

Chippendale, Thomas, 24

Churchill, Winston, 65, Plate 32

Cimex lectularius, 69, 76

Cockroaches, 68

Coleridge's Ancient Mariner, 77—8

Colnbrook, murder bed at, 58—61, Plates 26*a* and 26*b*

Composers who worked in bed, 65

Corot, J. B. C., Plate 43*b*

Cots. *See* Cradles

Courbet, Gustave, Plate 42*b*

Courting, 88*ff*

Coutts, Thomas, 38

Couvade, 47—50, Plate 20

Cradle, gods of, 47

Cradles, 53—5, *55*, 56, Plates 21—24

Crane at Colnbrook, 58—61

Cunnington, C. Willett, 36, 38

Dali, Salvador, Plate 60

David, Gerard, Plate 58

David, Jacques-Louis, Plate 42*a*

Day, James Wentworth, Plate 50

Death, 101—8, Plates 71*b*, 72*a* and 72*b*

Death-bed sayings, 104—7

Deffand, Marquise du, 106

Delacroix, F. V. E., Plate 39*b*
Delafosse, J. C., Plate 8
Deloney, Thomas, 58—61
De l'Orme, Charles, 57
Dickens, Charles, 33, Plate 70*a*
Dingwall, E. J., 99
Dinka, 17, 49
Diodorus, 48
Dior, Christian, Plate 53*b*
Donizetti, Gaetano, 65
Double beds, 35 *et passim*
Droit de seigneur, 94—5
Du Maurier, George, 33
Duval, Raoul, 73
Dying, art of, 101—8

Edward VII of England, Plate 72*b*
Egyptian beds, 18, Plates 3*a* and 3*b*
Electric blanket, 34
Elizabeth I of England, 24
English beds, 24 *et passim*, Plates 7, 9, 10, 11, and 15*b*
Eskimoes, 17

Fakirs, 28, Plate 16*b*
Famous last words, 104—7
Félice, Roger de, 75
Fertility rites, 46
Fetherstonhaugh, Harry, 64
Fleas, 68—9, *70—1*
Fontaine-Martel, Madame de, 106
Fosbroke, Thomas, 21, 30
Fosbrooke, Jonas, 58
Four-posters, 22 *et passim*
Fragonard, Jean Honoré, Plate 37*b*
François I of France, 41
Frazer, James G., 32, 33
French beds, 22—4, *23*, Plates 8, 12*a* and 12*b*
Frenchmen as lovers, 96

Gainsborough, Thomas, 62
Garrick, Mrs., 105
Gaskell, Elizabeth, 41
Géricault, J. L. A. T., Plates 40 and 41
German beds, 20, Plate 6
Gervex, Henri, Plate 44*b*
Gibbon, Edward, 40—1
Girdle of chastity, 98
Glinka, F. N., 65
Glycogen, 82
Goddess of Health. *See* Vestina, Hebe
Goncharov, Ivan, 67
Goya, Plate 39*a*
Grabatum, 21
Graham, Harvey, 64
Graham, James, 35, 39, 61—4, 97, Plate 27
Grationapolitanus, Hugo, 37
Gray, C. and M., 43, 66, 67, 103
Greek beds, 19, 35
Greville, Charles, 64
Guérin, P. N., Plate 54
Gyrgatus, 22

Hamilton, Emma, 64
Hamilton, William, 64
Hammock, 18, Plate 14*a*
Hare, Augustus, 67
Hart, Emma, 64
Hathaway, Anne, bed of, Plate 25
Havard, Henry, 23, *36*, 58, 74, 75
Hay fever, 72
Head-rests, 17—19, Plates 1*a*, 1*b*, 2*a*, 2*b* and 2*c*
Henry VII of England, 33, 92
Henry VIII of England, 37
Hepplewhite, George, 24
Hobbes, Thomas, 65, 106
Hogarth, William, Plates 19*b* and 70*b*
Holloway, Stanley, Plate 53*a*

Hospital beds, *102*, 103
Hot-water bottles, 34—5
Howard, Flavilla, 92
Howard, John, 50—1, Plate 19*b*
Hughes, Howard, 103
Huichol Indians, 46
Hunter, William, 106
Hyde, Anne, Duchess of York, 106
Hypnos, Plate 57*a*

Indian beds, 28, Plate 67*b*
Ingres, J. A. D., *Frontispiece*
Insomnia, 79—82
Irving, Washington, 90
Italian beds, 24, Plate 5*a*

Japanese beds, 28
Jezebel, 43
Jittery legs, 72
Johnson, Samuel, 42, 65
Josephine, Empress, bed of, Plate 29
Jus primae noctis, 94—5

Kleitman, Nathaniel, 82, 83

Lahontan, Baron, 96
Lake, Edward, 93
Lapp cradle, Plate 24*b*
Latour, Fantin, 66
Lecouvreur, Adrienne, 105
Lenin, 107
Leonardo da Vinci, 29
Lice, 68—9
Lieutaud, 106
Lincoln, Mary, 92
Lit à colonnes, 23
Lit à deux dossiers, 23
Lit à l'anglaise, 23
Lit clos, 23
Lit d'ange, 22
Lit de glace, 23

Lit de justice, 73, Plates 55 and 56*a*
Lit de parade, 73—6, Plates 54 and 56*b*
Lit en tombeau, 23
Louis XIV of France, 24
Louis XV of France, Plate 55
Love-making, 88—100, Plates 40, 41 and 67*a*; potency in, 96; excessive indulgence in, 97—8; at advanced age, 98
Ludwig II of Bavaria, 57
Lying-in, 44*ff*, 74
Lying in state, 75—6
Lyon, Emma, 64

Mackenzie, Compton, Plate 52
Maintenon, Marquise de, 24
Manet, Edouard, Plate 43*a*
Manningham, Richard, 51—2 Plate 19*b*
Margaret of Flanders, 54
Martinelli, Elsa, Plate 56*b*
Martins, Samuel, 65
Marx, Groucho, Mrs., 57
Matisse, Henri, Plate 46*a*
Mattresses, 20, 28—30
Mazurki, Mike, 53
Median beds, 18
Medieval beds, *19*, 20—1, *21*, *36*, Plates 4, 13*a*, 17, 18, 49, 58, 67*a* and 71*a*
Melville, Herman, 41
Mende, 32
Metternich, Prince, 26
Middle Ages, beds in. *See* Medieval beds
Modigliani, Amedeo, Plate 47
Montagu, Mary Wortley, 106
Montesquiou, Madame de, bed of, Plate 12*a*
More, Thomas, 37
Moufet, Thomas, 69

Moxos Indians, 32
Mundassas, 32
Murder-bed at Colnbrook, 58—61,
 Plates 26a and 26b
Music composed in bed, 65

Naples, Princess of, 92—3
Narcolepsy, 86
Nelson, Lord, 64
Night-cap, 38
Night-clothes, 36—9
Night-shirt, 37—8
Nuer, 17

Oblomovitis, 68—9, 86
Ostrich at Colnbrook, 59
Ovid, 99—100

Paisiello, Giovanni, 65
Palliasses, 20
Paradise Lost written in bed, 65
Parr, Thomas, 98
Peron, Eva, 107
Persian beds, 18
Philip the Good, bed of, 58
Phylarchus, 73
Pickwick, Mr., Plate 70a
Pillows, 17, 18, 30
Pincher, Chapman, 80
Plato, 43
Polo, Marco, 27, 48
Polynesian bed-mats, 17
Potency, 96—7
Pregnancy 44ff; superstitions con-
 cerning, 52—3
Propertius, 99
Pruritus, 72
Puccini, Giacomo, 65
Pulex irritans, 69, 76
Pyjamas, 38

Rabbits, Mary Toft gives birth to,
 50—2
Red Indians, bundling among, 90
Rembrandt, Plates 34 and 35
Renan, J. E., 107
Revivalists, American, on sex, 91—2
Reynolds, Reginald, 34, 40, 43, 50,
 57, 65, 73, 84, 103
Richelieu, Cardinal, 43
Roman bedding, 30
Roman beds, 19—21
Roper, William, 37
Rossini, G. A., 65
Rousseau, Jean-Jacques, 65
Rowlandson, Thomas, Plate 59b

St. André, Nathaniel, 50, Plate 19b
St. Remy, Le Fèvre de, 58
Saint-Simon, L. de, 43
Savage Alarum Bedstead, 86
Saxon beds, 20, 21
Saxon pillows, 30
Sceta, 30
Schiller, J. C. F. von, 106
Scympodium, 22
Sea Dyaks, bundling among, 90
Seduction, 88ff, Plates 66—70
Sex, 88—100
Shakespeare, William, 57, 77, 100
Sharing the bed, 35, 39—40
Shaw, Bernard, 107
Shaw, R. N., Plate 21
Sheets, 30—1
Sheraton, Thomas, 24, Plates 30 and
 31
Siesta, 66—7
Sleep, 77—87, Plates 57—65; cycles
 of, 82—3; protracted, 85—6;
 learning languages in, 84
Sleeping naked, 17, 20, 36—7
Sleeplessness, 82
Smith, Adam, 105

Snoring, 84
Solomon in bed, *19*
Southall, John, 69
Southwell, Martha, 85
Stiles, Henry Reed, 90
Stopes, Marie, 28, 30, 33—5, 39, 58,
    67, 81, 84
Stow, John, 84—5
Strabo, 48
Strauss, Richard, 100
Superstitions about beds and bed-
    ding, 32—3
Surrington, Joseph, 98
Sutherland, Halliday, 89
Swift, Jonathan, 65

Tchin-chan, 94
Temple of Health, 62—4
Thérèse, Marie, 24
Titian, Plate 36*a*
Toft, Mary, 50—2, Plate 19*b*
Toradjas, 53
Toulouse-Lautrec, Henri de, Plate
    33*a*
Tunis, bed of Bey of, Plate 28
Tut-Ankh-Amen, beds found in
    tomb of, 18, Plates 3*a* and 3*b*
Twain, Mark, 65

Umphreville, Lavinia, 91—2

Valadon, Suzanne, Plate 45
Valentino, Rudolf, 107
Vallotton, Félix, Plate 44*a*
Van Gogh, Vincent, Plate 33*b*
Vaughan, William, 38
Velasquez, Plate 36*b*
Vestina, Hebe, 63, Plate 27
Vinci, Leonardo da, 29
Viollet-le-Duc, Eugène E., *19*, 20
Voltaire, 65
Vuillard, Jean Edouard, Plate 46*b*

Wagner, Richard, 100
Ware, Great Bed of, 22, 57—8, Plate
    26*c*
Warming-pans, 34, Plate 59*b*
Watteau, Jean Antoine, Plate 38
Westermarck, Edward, 94
Wheels, bed on, *21*
Whittington, Dick, death of, Plate
    71*b*
Wilde, Oscar, 107
William IV of England, cradle of,
    55
Witkowski, G. J. A., *44*, *45*, *55*, *102*
Wordsworth, William, 77

Xenophon, 18

Young, Edward, 77

Head-rests

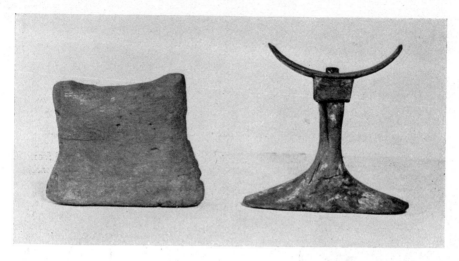

(*a*) Two ancient Egyptian head-rests. *Horniman Museum, London*

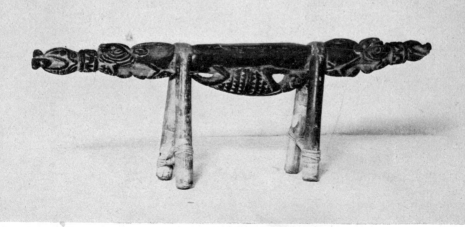

(*b*) A head-rest of carved wood from New Guinea. *Horniman Museum, London*

PLATE 1

(*a*) A double head-rest in wood from South Africa. *Horniman Museum, London*

(*b*) A grotesquely carved wooden head-rest from New Guinea. *Horniman Museum, London*

(*c*) A child's stuffed head-rest from China. The wide-open eyes keep watch during the night hours. *Horniman Museum, London*

PLATE 2

Beds Through the Ages

(*a*) and (*b*) This ancient Egyptian folding bed, made in the fourteenth century B. C., was part of the treasure found by Howard Carter and Lord Carnarvon in the tomb of Tut-Ankh-Amen at Thebes. A closely woven linen string web is stretched across the wooden frame, and the legs, of feline shape, rest upon copper drums. *Egyptian Museum, Cairo*

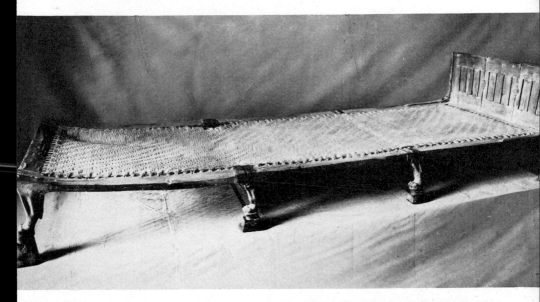

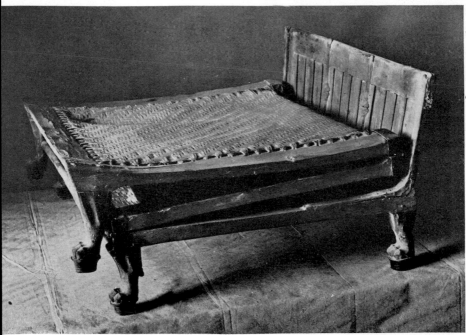

PLATE 3

Medieval beds were often of very simple and comfortless design. This example is typical of the early fifteenth century

PLATE 4

(*a*) An Italian bed of the late fifteenth century as depicted in the Vision of St. Ursula, by Vittore Carpaccio (*fl.* 1490). *Accademia, Venice*

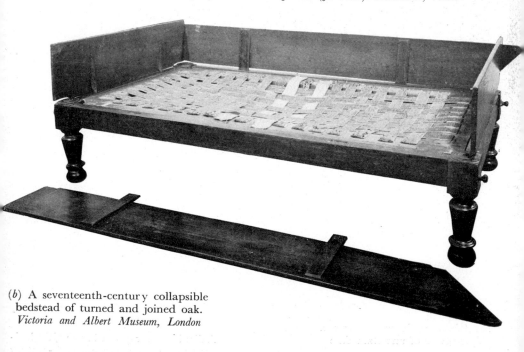

(*b*) A seventeenth-century collapsible bedstead of turned and joined oak.
Victoria and Albert Museum, London

PLATE 5

An elaborately decorated German
four-poster of uncertain date

PLATE 6

PLATE 7 (*opposite*)
A dignified four-poster in one of the bed-
rooms at Uppark, a seventeenth-century
mansion near Petersfield, Hampshire

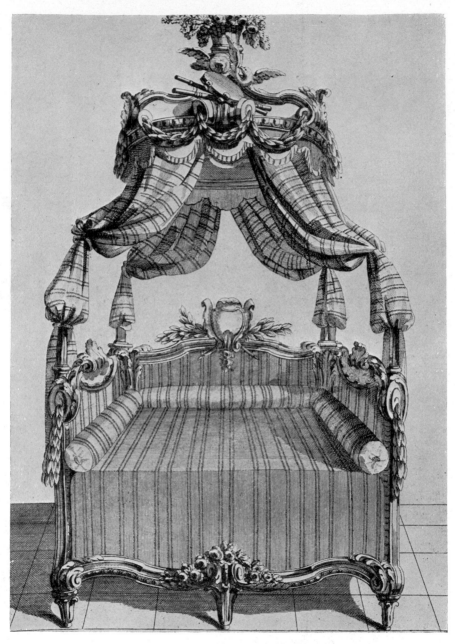

Lit à la Polonaise by Jean Charles Delafosse (1734—1789)

PLATE 8

English chinoiserie at its most elegant. A lacquered and gilt bedstead from Badminton, Gloucestershire. About 1760. *Victoria and Albert Museum, London*

PLATE 9

A canopied bedstead shown at the Great Exhibition of 1851

PLATE 10

This English *papier mâché* bed of about 1860 was given to the Victoria and
Albert Museum by H.M. Queen Mary

PLATE 11

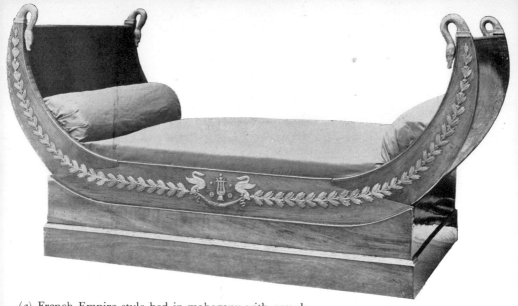

(*a*) French Empire-style bed in mahogany with ormulu mounts, said to have been given by Napoleon I to Mademoiselle de Montesquiou, governess to the King of Rome. It later belonged to the artist Whistler. *Victoria and Albert Museum, London*

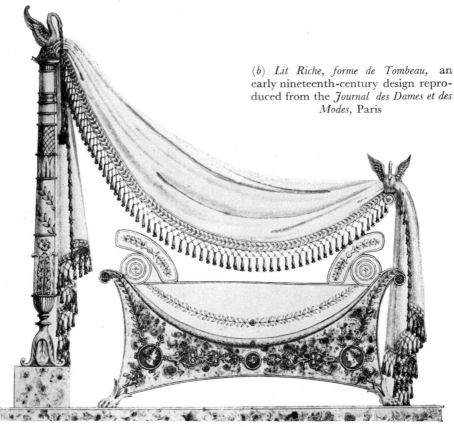

(*b*) *Lit Riche, forme de Tombeau,* an early nineteenth-century design reproduced from the *Journal des Dames et des Modes,* Paris

PLATE 12

PLATE 13

Unusual Beds

(a) A medieval sloping bedstead of rope and metal. *From Viollet-le-Duc (1855—8), Vol. 1, p. 172*

(b) (below) A nobleman reclining on his travelling bed. *From Viollet-le-Duc (1855—8), Vol .1, facing p. 190*

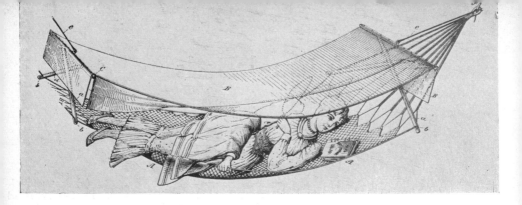

(*a*) A mechanized hammock of the 'nineties. Cross-bracing holds the net at the proper tension while the occupant relaxes beneath a sheltering device with her fan and poems á la mode. *U.S. Patent 495,532, 18 April 1893*

PLATE 14

(*b*) A monumental bed in solid silver built for an Indian prince. The life-size statues at each corner are in natural colour with enamel eyes and wigs of real hair. When the Maharajah lay down, his weight started a musical box hidden in the mattress, while the statues waved their fans and fly-whisks. The bed weighs over a ton. *Christofle, Paris*

(*a*) Mattresses have often been stuffed with straw, but today a natural bed in a hayloft is rather more unusual: two art students on a touring holiday

PLATE 15

(*b*) 'The Electronic Road to Ritzy Relaxation.' This luxurious modern bed, costing £ 2,500, is described on p. 26. It was first shown at the Furniture Exhibition at Earls Court, London, in 1959

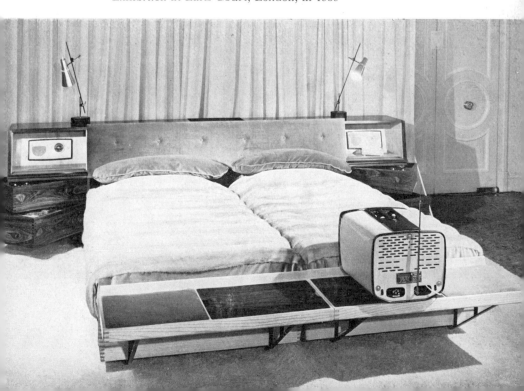

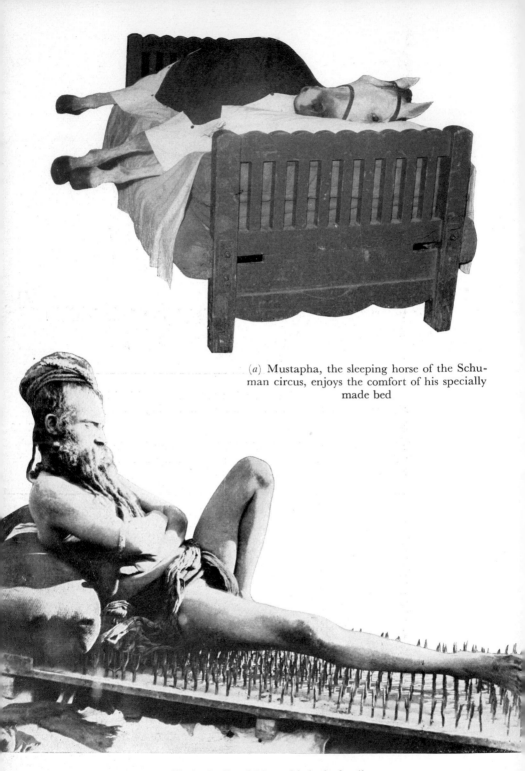

(*a*) Mustapha, the sleeping horse of the Schu-
man circus, enjoys the comfort of his specially
made bed

(*b*) An Indian fakir on his bed of nails

PLATE 16

Birth

The Nativity, with St. Joseph and nurse. French, fifteenth century.
From Add. MS. 18192, f. 52, British Museum, London

PLATE 17

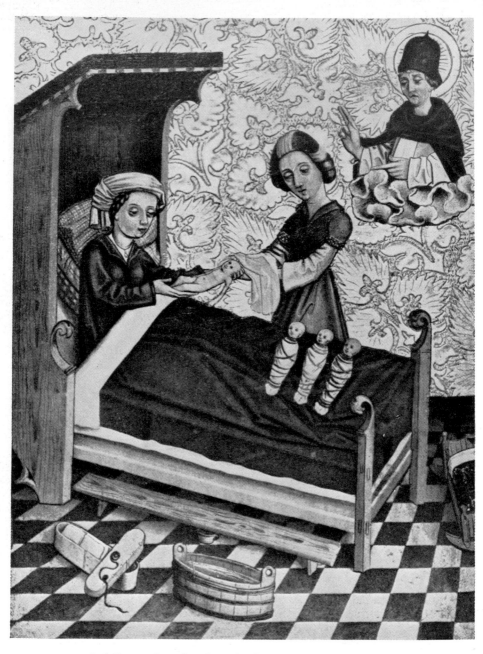

A delivery of quadruplets, the first three already wrapped in swaddling clothes (see pp. 52—3). From a medieval manuscript, *c*. 1450.
Oberrheinische Schule

PLATE 18

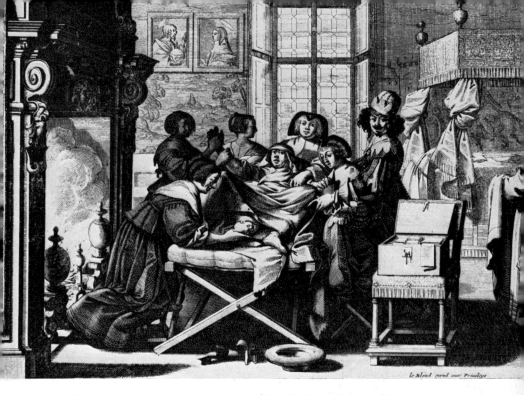

(*a*) The delivery of a fine boy. Engraved by Abraham Bosse, *c.* 1630

PLATE 19

(*b*) Mary Toft giving birth to rabbits, by Hogarth. A: St. André. B: Manningham. C: Vet. D: Howard. E: Toft. F: Mary Toft. G: Nurse (see pp. 49—51). *From St. André (1727), frontispiece*

Couvade (see pp. 46—8). *From a Chinese MS. album in the Victoria and Albert Museum, London*

PLATE 20

PLATE 21

Cots and Cradles

An English oak cradle, decorated with birds and the signs of the
Zodiac, by Richard Norman Shaw (1831–1912). *Victoria and Albert
Museum, London*

An early-nineteenth-century French cradle in
mahogany with ormolu mounts. *Victoria and Albert
Museum, London*

PLATE 22

PLATE 23 (*opposite*)
The cot of the infant King of Rome
now in the Château of Fontainbleau

(*a*) 'A swing cot-bed for an
infant.' *Ackermann's Repository,
September 1809, London*

(*b*) A Lapp mother tends her baby in its simple wooden cradle

PLATE 24

Some Notable Beds

Anne Hathaway's bed in her cottage at Stratford-on-Avon

PLATE 25

PLATE 26

(*a*) and (*b*) Two views of a model by F. J. Camm and others of the murder bed at the Ostrich, Colnbrook (see pp. 58—61)

(*c*) The Great Bed of Ware (see pp. 57—8). *Victoria and Albert Museum, London*

Hebe Vestina, the Rosy Goddess of Health, reclining on one of the beds in Dr. James Graham's Temple of Health and of Hymen (see pp. 61—4)

PLATE 27

The bed of the former Bey of Tunis in the Bardo Palace, Tunis

PLATE 28

The bed of the Empress Josephine (1763—1814)

PLATE 29

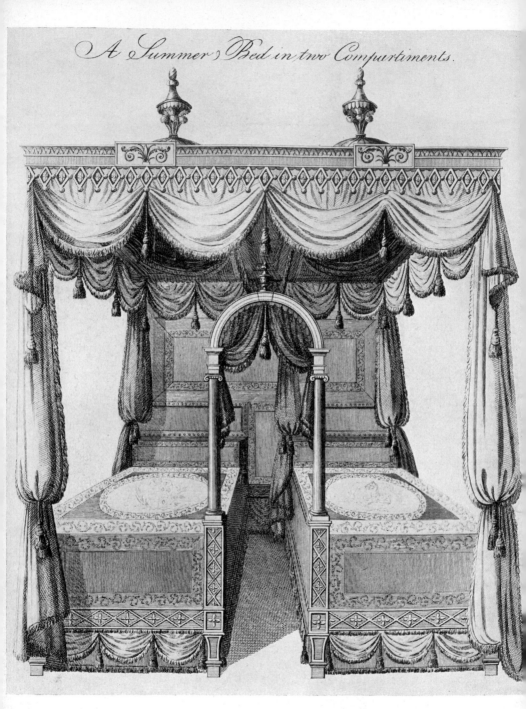

'A Summer Bed in two Compartiments', by Thomas Sheraton. *From The Cabinet-Maker und Upholsterer's Drawing Book, 1802*

PLATE 30

'An eliptic bed for a single lady'—another revolutionary Sheraton design

PLATE 31

The room in Blenheim Palace where Sir Winston Churchill was born
on November 30th, 1874

PLATE 32

(*a*) The Bed, by Toulouse-Lautrec (1864—1901). *Louvre, Paris*

The Bed in Art

PLATE 33

(*b*) The Painter's Bedroom, by Van Gogh (1853—1890).
Collection V. W. Van Gogh, Laren

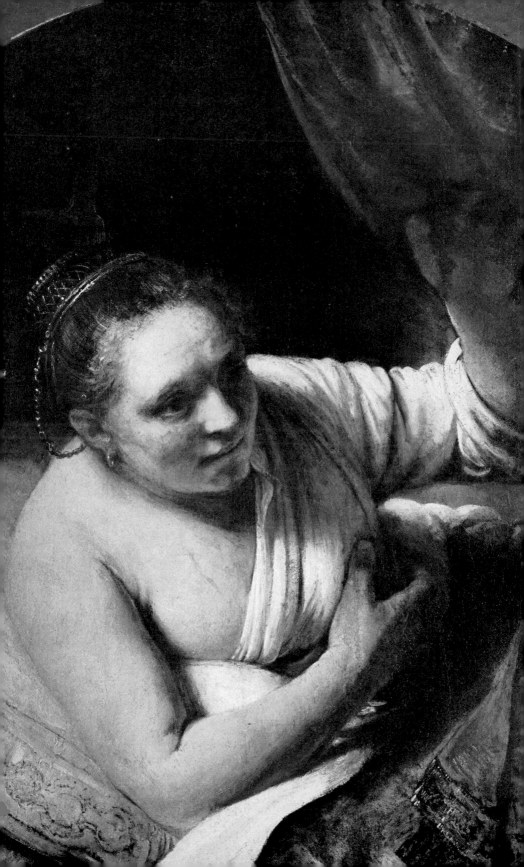

Danaë, by Rembrandt (1606—1669). *Hermitage, Leningrad*

PLATE 35

(*a*) The Venus of Madrid, by Titian (1477—1576). *Prado, Madrid*

PLATE 36

(*b*) Venus and Cupid ('The Rokeby Venus'), by Velasquez (1599—1660). *National Gallery, London*

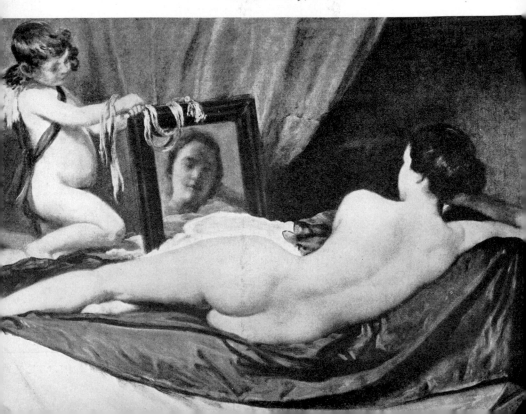

(*a*) Miss Morphise O'Murphy, by Boucher (1703–1770). *Kunsthistorisches Museum, Vienna*

(*b*) The Beautiful
Serving Maid by
Fragonard (1732–1806).
Nationalmuseum, Stockholm

PLATE 37

The Secret Toilet, by Watteau (1684—1721). *Private Collection, Paris*

PLATE 38

(*a*) Maya Naked, by Goya (1746—1828). *Prado, Madrid*

(*b*) Nude with
White Stockings,
by Delacroix
(1798—1863).
Louvre, Paris

PLATE 39

Overleaf) PLATES 40 and 41 The Kiss, by Géricault (1791—1824). *Private collection, London*

(*a*) Cupid and Psyche, by Jacques-Louis David (1748–1825).
Private collection, Paris

PLATE 42

(*b*) Sleep, by Courbet (1819–1877). *Petit Palais, Paris*

Nude, by Suzanne Valadon (1867—1938). *Collection de la Ville de Paris*

PLATE 45

(*a*) Odalisque, by Matisse (1869—1954). *Musée National d'Art Moderne, Paris*

PLATE 46

(*b*) In Bed, by Vuillard (1868—1940). *Musée National d'Art Moderne, Paris*

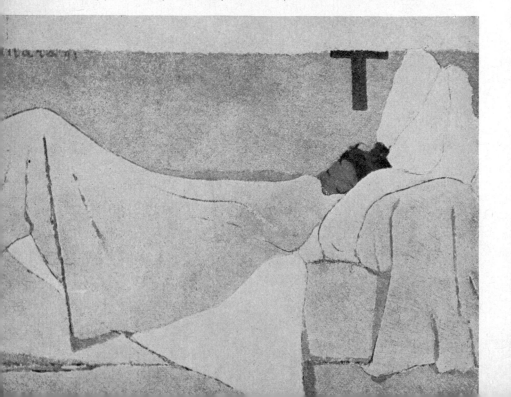

Nude, by Modigliani (1884—1920). *Musées Royaux des Beaux-Arts, Antwerp*

(*Overleaf*) PLATE 48 The Man and the Woman, by Pierre Bonnard (1867—1947). *Musée National d'Art Moderne, Paris*

PLATE 47

Lying in Bed

Lying on a medieval sloping bed. *From Harl. MS. 4373, f. 88v, British Museum, London*

PLATE 49

Well-known sportsman and journalist James Wentworth Day faces
a new dawn in his comfortable four-poster

PLATE 50

Actress Agnes Bernelle relaxes in a richly carved seventeenth-century
four-poster

PLATE 51

Sir Compton Mackenzie reflects on his early-morning mail

PLATE 52

PLATE 53 (*opposite*)

(*a*) *top*. Actor Stanley Holloway trying over a part to his son

(*b*) *bottom*. The late Christian Dior at breakfast

Lit de Parade and
Lit de Justice

For an account of these ceremonial aspects of lying in bed
the reader should turn to page 73

Dido on her *lit de parade* listens as Aeneas recounts the misfortunes
of Troy. From the painting by Pierre Narcisse Guérin (1774—
1883). *Louvre, Paris*

PLATE 54

Louis XV of France on his *lit de justice*. From Havard (1887—90),
Vol. 3, facing columns 423 and 424

PLATE 55

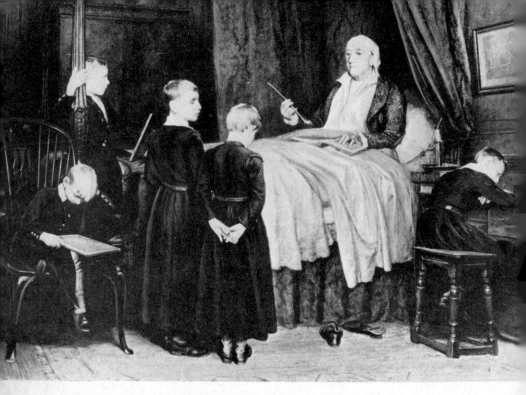

(*a*) Tuition at Dulwich College in the early nineteenth century provided a special example of the *lit de justice*. From a picture painted by W. C. Horsley in 1828. *Dulwich College, London*

PLATE 56

(*b*) Italian actress Elsa Martinelli receives her director and publicity men on her *lit de parade* at the Savoy Hotel, London

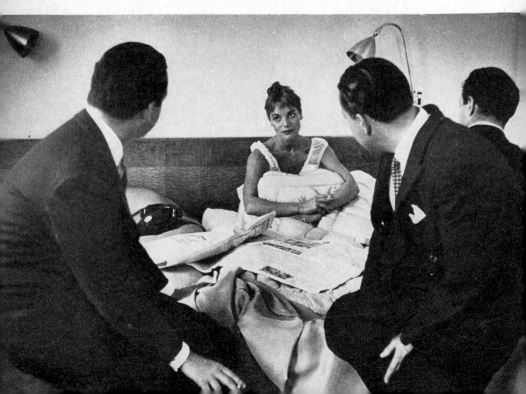

(*a*) Bronze head of Hypnos, the Greek personification of sleep. *British Museum, London*

Sleep

(*b*) Tobias and Sara asleep. German stained glass, *c*. 1530. *Victoria and Albert Museum, London*

PLATE 57

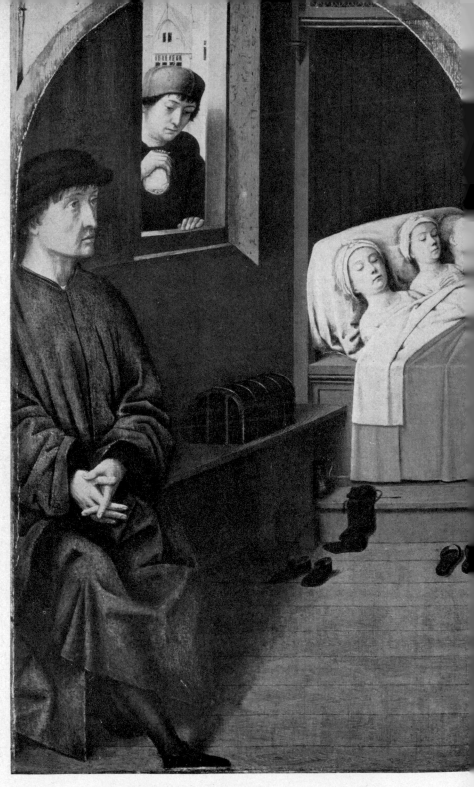

St. Nicholas bestows a dowry on the three daughters of
an impoverished father. From the picture by Gerard David
(c. 1450—1523). *National Gallery of Scotland, Edinburgh*

PLATE 58

(*a*) Three chorus girls on tour in theatrical 'digs'—perhaps dreaming of a modern St. Nicholas (*see* Plate 58)

(*b*) A rude awakening for a guest in an eighteenth-century inn, when the chambermaid mistakes his wooden leg for the handle of a warming-pan. Print by Thomas Rowlandson (1756—1827)

PLATE 59

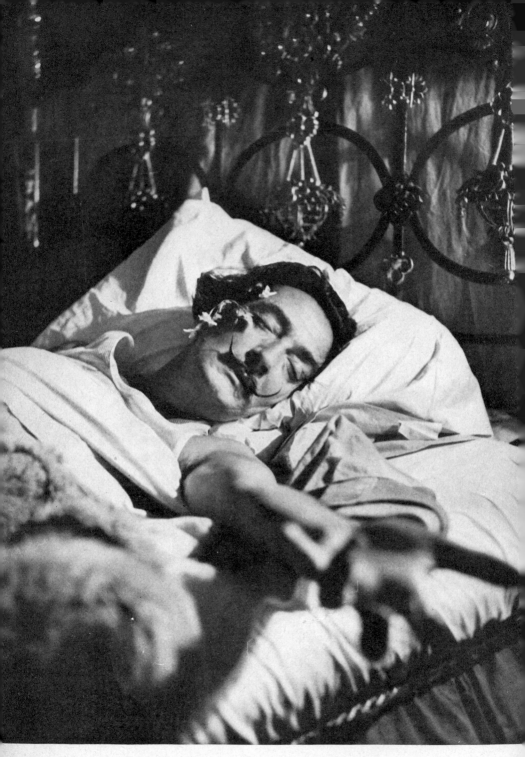

Spanish painter Salvador Dali

PLATE 60

Irish dramatist, the late Brendan Behan

PLATE 61

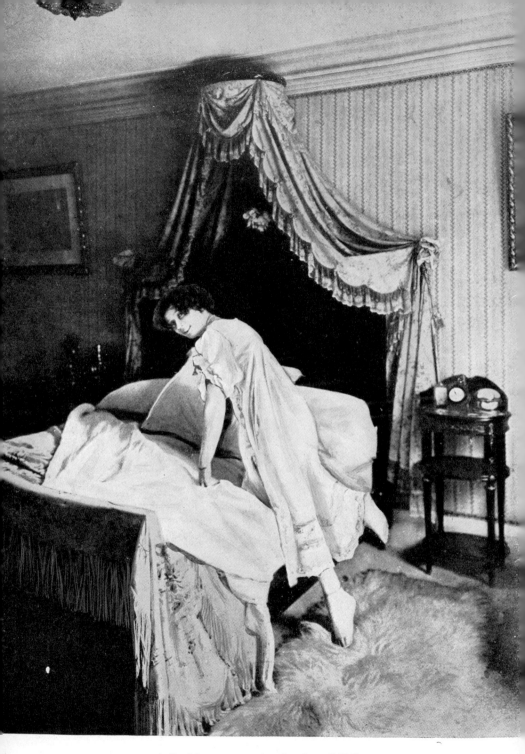

A Parisienne preparing for sleep (1912)

PLATE 62

A Londoner preparing for sleep (1940)

PLATE 63

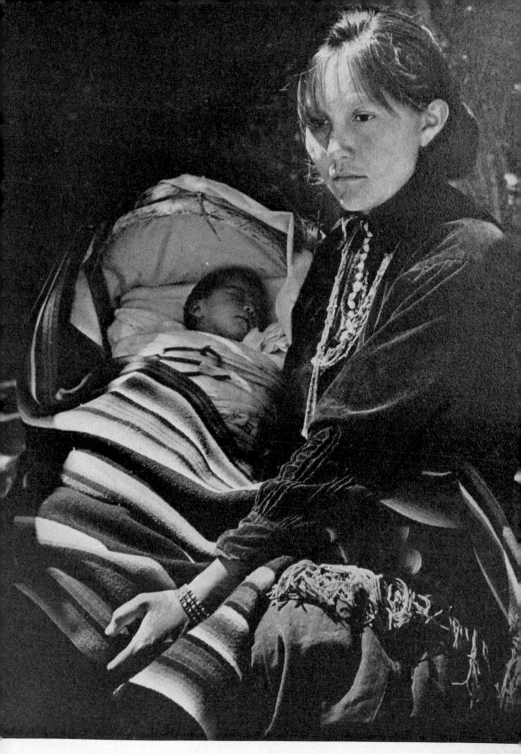

The papoose of a Navajo squaw sleeps peacefully in the security of its cradle

PLATE 64 *(opposite)*
A hard bed in a hard world: Shaftesbury Avenue, London   PLATE 65

Seduction and Love-making

Invitation to a bed of reeds. From a French postcard entitled *La Source*

PLATE 66

(a) The conception of Alexander: Nectanebus (right) as a dragon reassumes his human shape for the seduction of Olimpias. *From Royal MS. 15.e.vi, British Museum, London*

PLATE 67

(b) A prince dallying with ladies on a bed: an Indian miniature painted about 1720. *Victoria and Albert Museum, London*

The Favourite Lover: an engraving by Chaponnier after the French
genre and portrait painter Louis Léopold Boilly (1761—1845).
Victoria and Albert Museum, London

PLATE 68

The Intrigue Discovered. A late eighteenth-century French engraving.
Victoria and Albert Museum, London

PLATE 69

PLATE 70

(*a*) Mr. Pickwick surprised in the wrong room by 'a middle-aged lady in yellow curl-papers'. Illustration by Phiz to the *Pickwick Papers* by Charles Dickens

(*b*) (*below*) A Hogarth engraving showing 'The Idle Prentice returned from sea and in a Garret with a common Prostitute' *Victoria and Albert Museum, London*

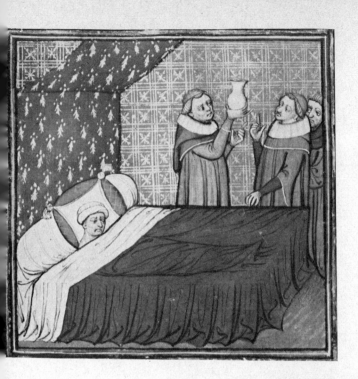

Sickness and Death

(*a*) Illness of John, Duke of Normandy: two doctors examine his urine. *From Royal MS. 20.c.vii, 78b, (French, c. 1320), British Museum, London*

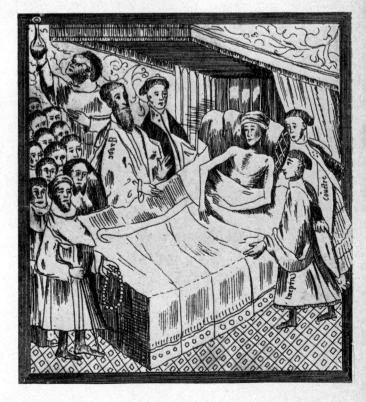

(*b*) The Death of Dick Whittington. *From Londinium Redivivum, by J. P. Malcolm, London, 1807, facing p. 515*

PLATE 71

(*a*) Prince Albert, the Prince Consort, on his deathbed in 1861

(*b*) King Edward VII lying in state in 1910

PLATE 72